NVQ/ SVQ LEVEL 3

Managing Operations

A COMPETENCE APPROACH TO SUPERVISORY MANAGEMENT

T0369632

Foreword from the MCI

Roger Cartwright • Michael Collins
George Green • Anita Candy

BLACKWELL
Business

IN CHARGE

First published 1993

Reprinted 1996

Blackwell Publishers Ltd
108 Cowley Road
Oxford OX4 1JF, UK

Blackwell Publishers Inc.
238 Main Street
Cambridge, Massachusetts 02142, USA

British Library Cataloguing in Publication Data
A CIP catalogue record for this book is available from the British Library

Library of Congress Cataloging in Publication Data has been applied for.

ISBN   0–631–19011–2

Typeset in 11.5 on 14pt Palatino
by Joshua Associates Ltd, Oxford

This book is printed on acid-free paper

Managing Operations

In Charge
Series Editor: Roger Cartwright

Contents

List of Figures

Foreword

In pursuit of its strategy to improve the performance of UK organizations by improving the quality of their managers, MCI have developed competence-based management standards for practical use and as a basis for assessment for vocational awards.

In focusing at the supervisory management level, this book provides a simple and practical way of acquiring knowledge and understanding in preparation for the development of those standards, thus providing the first step in career progression for those aspiring to a managerial career.

The abundant case samples drawn from practical experience illustrate the elements of supervisory management activity which require achievement in most organizations. This book is heartily commended to all candidates seeking to develop such qualifications and offers a background to providers, employers and candidates to progress towards the achievement of their organization's objectives.

Vlad Stanić
Development Director
Management Charter Initiative

For June, Yvonne, Bronwen and Philip

We would like to express our grateful thanks to all those who have provided help and criticism during the preparation of the volumes of *In Charge*, especially to Blackwell Publishers and their reviewers – Donna Green of Rover Group, Jane Hawkins of NEBSM Regional Managers, Evelyn Lee-Barber of Bass plc, Sandy Milton of the Radcliffe Infirmary Oxford, and Terry Guy and Debbie Stones of Autotype International.

Jean walked out of the door trying to control her breathing. She hadn't known why Mr Raymond wanted to see her, although she didn't think that she'd done anything wrong.

When he offered her the vacant position of section supervisor (vacant because Jim had moved to the new offices) on a temporary basis pending the outcome of the current organizational review, she was filled with a mixture of thoughts:

> The money would be useful

> What about the responsibility?

> What would the staff think?

> How much extra time would it take?

She asked about Alan and Maureen who were both senior to her, but Mr Raymond had said that Alan was taking up an offer of early retirement and Maureen wanted a job share that was on offer in another department

She'd accepted the position but as she walked down the corridor one question above all others kept coming back into her mind:

'He's told me I'm going to be *In Charge* . . . but what does that actually mean?'

Introduction

This introduction to *In Charge, Managing Operations* is a summary of chapters 1–3 of *In Charge* volume 1, *Managing People*.

- What the series is about
- Who the series is intended for
- Programmes for which the volumes will be useful
- Scope of the volumes
- How to use the volumes
- Supervisors and managers – what's in a title?
- What is management competence?
- The management standards
- Demonstrating competence
- Competence audit
- Personal competences

WHAT THE SERIES IS ABOUT

The three volumes in this series are designed to provide those in supervisory and first line management positions with the knowledge and skills to carry out their supervisory and management tasks with competence.

WHO THE SERIES IS INTENDED FOR

If you have responsibilities for others within your organization or you are seeking such responsibility, you will find this series useful. You may have been in your post for some time, you may have been promoted recently or you may be seeking promotion: in all these cases, this series will provide you with useful knowledge and understanding to support you within the work situation and will aid you with your managerial/supervisory and personal development.

The series is intended to be equally relevant to all areas of work and contains cases from the private, public and voluntary sectors.

The series will also provide useful material for those responsible for training at this level, and has been specially designed to support National Vocational Qualification (NVQ) or Scottish Vocational Qualification (SVQ) programmes at Level 3 supervisory management.

PROGRAMMES FOR WHICH THE VOLUMES WILL BE USEFUL

In Charge has been written to support supervisory/first line management (FLM) development programmes at NVQ or SVQ Level 3 in addition to company short courses and individual development.

Such courses, validated by BTEC, ISM and NEBSM, are offered by a large number of further education establishments and open learning providers.

SCOPE OF THE VOLUMES

The areas covered are:

Volume 1 *Managing People*

This volume commences by looking at how ideas of supervision and management have developed over time and then considers how to manage people effectively. It covers: motivation; human reactions to change; recruitment, selection and training; working with teams and groups; leadership; handling conflict; and concludes with a consideration of the role of the supervisor/first line manager in the discipline and grievance process.

Volume 2 *Managing Operations*

This volume looks at the operations of an organization and the part played by supervisors and junior managers. The volume examines the different types of organizations you will encounter – public sector, private sector, etc. – and considers the relationship between operations and other organizational functions, such as marketing and personnel. The volume then examines the operations function in more detail, covering work practices, planning, resourcing, legislation (e.g. HSAW) and customer relations.

Volume 3 *Managing Finance and Information*

This volume covers two key areas of supervision and first line management. Managing information examines the types of information the supervisor/first line manager is likely to encounter and considers ways of disseminating and presenting such information. The finance section is designed to give the reader a broad overview of the role finance plays in an organization; it is not intended to turn the reader into an accountant, but rather to provide the supervisor/FLM with an understanding of financial language and practices as they relate to the work situation.

HOW TO USE THE VOLUMES

No set of books, however well written, can provide the answer to a specific problem that an individual has encountered. However, by providing the individual with an insight into the processes that are at work within situations, and with opportunities to examine situations from a variety of standpoints, books such as those in the *In Charge* series can allow the supervisor/first line manager to make more informed decisions.

Use the volumes as you would a handbook: scan through first to gain the flavour of the subject, and then home in on specifics. The volumes form an integrated package, and while each can stand alone, at the same time they support each other and refer you backwards and forwards. Supervision and first line management tasks cannot be pigeon-holed into purely managing people or solely managing finance, and neither can an effective supporting text.

SUPERVISORS AND MANAGERS – WHAT'S IN A TITLE?

Supervisor	Foreman
Chargehand	Senior . . . .
First Line Manager	NCO (Armed Forces)

Junior Manager	Assistant Manager
Trainee Manager	Team Leader
Coordinator	Administrator
Section Leader	Staff Nurse

Organizations within the United Kingdom display little consistency in the titles given to those working in supervisory/junior management positions. One company may consider a person to be a supervisor while another company may designate a similar post 'assistant manager'; it all depends on the type of company, the way in which positions have evolved, and industry custom and practice.

WHAT IS MANAGEMENT COMPETENCE?

The *Concise Oxford Dictionary* defines 'competent' as:

(a) adequately qualified or capable
(b) effective

How does one judge effectiveness or capability? The traditional approach to management/supervisory development was based upon standardized inputs: a set course of study, knowledge workshops etc., followed by some form of away-from-work examination. This form of development was able to test how much the participant had understood the concepts but was unable to test for them in actual work situations.

A competence approach uses evidence gained either from the work place or from work-related simulations to measure the effectiveness not of the learning but of the actual participant. To accomplish this requires a set of national standards against which competence can be measured.

A good example of a competence approach is the driving test. The examiner judges each person against a set of national criteria. How a person learned to drive is unimportant: the test measures whether they are a competent driver on the day.

However, to drive competently requires more than just undertaking a short test; it also requires knowledge and understanding (hence the Highway Code test). People taking their test do not normally do so using the exact right turns, parking exercises etc., that they practised on. They need the understanding necessary to transfer from practice exercises to those on the test.

THE MANAGEMENT STANDARDS

The competence of a supervisor or manager can be measured against national standards, like those that apply in the case of a driving test.

The Management Charter Initiative (MCI) is the lead body for developing management standards in the United Kingdom. At the time of writing (1992), standards have been developed at three levels:

M2	(NVQ/SVQ5)	for more senior managers
M1	(NVQ/SVQ4)	for junior/middle managers
M1 (Subset)	(NVQ/SVQ3)	for supervisors/first line managers

The standards allow a person to judge their competence in an objective manner by the way in which their performance matches up to the national criteria.

Because the standards are based more on what a person does than on what they know, they are of equal use to those undertaking a course of study and those who only wish to know more about their own effectiveness.

The standards are arranged in four key role areas:

Managing people
Managing operations
Managing information
Managing finance

The supervisory standards include a limited consideration of the management of finance within the operations role, as it is appreciated that supervisors/FLMs may have little day-to-day contact with the finance functions. Finance is included within the *In Charge* series in its own right in the volume *Managing Finance and Information*, because it is believed that those entering supervision and management will need a fuller appreciation of the role finance plays within their organization.

Each key role area is divided into a number of units which are further divided into elements of competence. Figure 0.1 summarizes the Supervisory Management Standards produced by the MCI.

The elements contain a series of performance criteria and range statements relating to that element. Performance criteria specify the outcomes a competent supervisor/FLM should achieve, and range

Unit 1 Maintain services and operations to meet quality standards

- Element 1.1 Maintain services and operations
- Element 1.2 Maintain the necessary conditions for an effective and safe work environment

Unit 2 Contribute to the planning, monitoring and control of resources

- Element 2.1 Plan for the use of resources
- Element 2.2 Monitor and control the use of resources

Unit 3 Contribute to the provision of personnel

- Element 3.1 Contribute to the identification of personnel requirements
- Element 3.2 Contribute to the selection of personnel

Unit 4 Contribute to the training and development of teams, individuals and self to enhance performance

- Element 4.1 Contribute to planning the training and development of teams and individuals
- Element 4.2 Contribute to training and development activities for teams and individuals
- Element 4.3 Contribute to the assessment of teams and individuals against training and development objectives
- Element 4.4 Develop oneself within the job

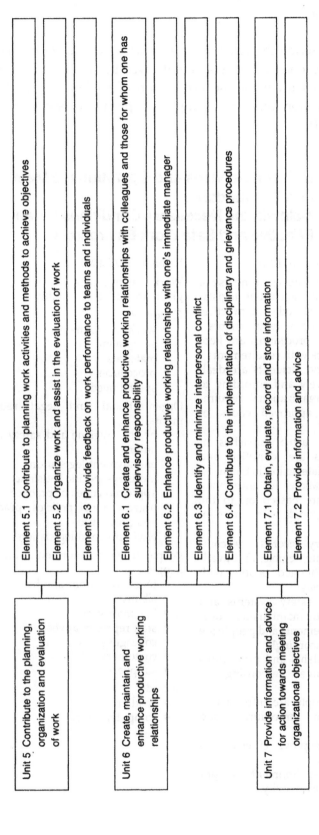

Figure 0.1 The structure of Supervisory Management Standards
Permission from MCI.

statements describe the circumstances within which the element is applied. These criteria and statements will be readily available to those who need them for the production of evidence as part of a formal qualification, and one example is reproduced below (permission from MCI).

Unit 1 Maintain Services and Operations to Meet Quality Standards
Element 1.2 Maintain the Necessary Conditions for an Effective and Safe Work Environment

PERFORMANCE CRITERIA

(a) Working conditions and the use of resources satisfy current legislation, approved codes of practice, and organizational requirements
(b) Maintenance procedures are kept in accordance with requirements
(c) Accidents and incidents are dealt with effectively and according to legal and organizational requirements and approved codes of practice
(d) Potential or actual breaches of requirements are identified and the appropriate action is taken
(e) Recommendations for improving conditions are passed on to the appropriate people with minimum delay
(f) All necessary records are complete, accurate, legible, and available to authorized people with minimum delay
(g) Health and safety systems and procedures are maintained according to requirements and people are instructed accordingly
(h) Security systems and procedures are maintained according to requirements
(i) Relevant people are informed of changes in procedures and requirements
(j) Action to improve efficiency is taken
(k) The work environment is conducive to work activity

RANGE STATEMENTS

Work environment is that within given area of responsibility

Conditions:
- work environment
- equipment
- materials
- procedures
- special needs

Organizational and legal requirements:
- health, hygiene and safety legislation
- employment legislation
- industry-specific legislation
- approved codes of practice
- organizational policies, practices and procedures
- environmental legislation

People to be kept informed/authorized people:
- those for whom one has responsibility
- line managers
- staff representatives
- colleagues
- customers
- suppliers

Records
- written
- computer-based

EVIDENCE SPECIFICATIONS

Sources of Evidence:

Performance at work over a period of time to cover all categories of range.

Where the candidate does not have the opportunity to cover all categories of range within the work place, evidence may be supplemented by oral questioning for understanding of basic principles and 'What if' scenarios. Evidence from related achievements outside the current work place may also be used.

Forms of Evidence:

Direct observation, products and outputs of performance e.g. legal documentation, statistics, reports, personal report, witness testimony.

DEMONSTRATING COMPETENCE

How do you demonstrate competence? In the main you can only demonstrate that you are competent at a task by carrying out that task to a defined standard. The *In Charge* series is designed around the Supervisory Management Standards.

There are only two states attached to competence:

Competent – having provided sufficient evidence of competency
Not yet competent – having provided insufficient evidence of competence

Those in the latter category are working towards competence.

An important feature of the Management Standards is their applicability across jobs: the same standards apply in public, private and voluntary sector firms and organizations. The tasks and context of the tasks change but the managerial competences remain as a constant.

Each volume of *In Charge* commences with a 'competence audit' to allow the reader to assess what it is they do and their competence at it based on the National Standards. The 'competence audit' asks you to look at each element of the Management Standards and to consider whether you do that task in your current job, or have done it in a previous job, and how competent you feel you really are.

You should now examine and complete the competence audit for *Managing Operations*, which is reproduced in figure 0.2.

Unit/Element	Do I do this in my job?			Have I ever done this in a job?			How competent do I feel I am?		
	O	S	N	O	S	N	V	P	N
1 Maintain services and operations to meet quality standards									
1.1 Maintain services and operations									
1.2 Maintain the necessary conditions for an effective and safe work environment									
2 Contribute to the planning, monitoring and control of resources									
2.1 Plan for the use of resources									
2.2 Monitor and control the use of resources									
5 (part of) Contribute to the planning, organization and evaluation of work									
5.1 Contribute to planning work activities and methods to achieve objectives									
5.2 Organize work and assist in the evaluation of work									

For task: O = often   S = sometimes   N = never
For competency: V = very   P = partially   N = not very

Figure 0.2 The Managing Operations Competence Audit

PERSONAL COMPETENCES

The competence standards we have looked at relate to the functions the supervisor/first line manager carries out. They can be considered as **functional competences**, i.e. as directly related to the job the supervisor/first line manager does. There are also a set of competences that relate to the personal attributes needed to be a competent manager at any level, ranging from supervisor to senior manager. These are known as **personal competences**.

The *In Charge* series covers both functional and personal competences. Each volume contains information on the personal competences and the functional competences to which they are linked.

Chapter 1

Setting Operations in Context

Supervisory Management Standards:

Unit 1   Maintain services and operations to meet quality standards

Element 1.1 Maintain services and operations

Unit 2   Contribute to the planning, monitoring and control of resources

Element 2.1 Plan for the use of resources

Unit 5   Contribute to the planning, organization and evaluation of work

Element 5.1 Contribute to planning work activities and methods to achieve objectives.

Case Note 1

Jane Thompson went into the lounge with an armful of linen and a tray in her hand. This was a job she hated – setting out the sugar bowls on the tables and generally ensuring that the room looked good. This morning, for some reason, people seemed to be ready for their coffee earlier than usual and there were already two couples sitting in the lounge, one already drinking and the other waiting for their order to arrive. Jane had just started to set a table when another couple entered, smiled at her and sat down in the corner. The woman held a rolled up brochure in her hand. Jane breathed a deep sigh and looked around at all the tables that were still do be done. If people kept arriving at this rate she would never be finished. She looked over at the new arrivals and said 'I'll be with you in just a minute'. Just time to get at least a few more tables done before I take their order, she thought.

In the corner, the woman had unfurled the brochure and was reading it. 'According to the write-up in here this is one of the top hotels in the area. It's got a swimming pool, gymnasium, lovely rooms and an excellent chef.'

'I noticed the menu up at the door when we came in, it certainly looks good,' her husband replied. 'Perhaps we should have lunch here too.'

'Well, let's see what the coffee's like and make our decision then. That's if anyone comes to take our order.'

She looked over towards the other corner of the room where Jane was still busy setting tables.

Jane looked at her watch. Nearly eleven o'clock. The whole room should have been ready by now and there were still ten tables left to do. Suddenly she remembered the couple who had just come in; she'd forgotten about them. Just one more table and she'd go and take their order, then while it was being prepared she could do the rest of the tables and might even be finished by the time it came to serve . . . that is, as long as no other customers came in to hold her up.

She finished the table and looked round towards the corner where the couple were sitting. There was no one there.

THE IMPORTANCE OF THE CUSTOMER

Have you ever stopped to think why you're working on a particular task?

In our hotel, Jane Thompson has been given some jobs to do, to set the tables ready for customers and to serve them coffee when they come in. There is no doubt that she is working hard at it and no one can doubt her efforts.

THINK POINT

However, if you were her supervisor, would you be satisfied with her performance?

So far she has one set of presumably satisfied customers who are drinking their coffee, another couple who are still waiting for it to be served and a further couple have left without buying anything. To make matters worse, the couple who left had arrived with very high hopes and were considering buying lunch in the restaurant.

It is very easy to become so preoccupied with a particular task that you are performing that you may forget the original reason for doing it. Here, Jane's prime objectives should be to serve coffee and thus satisfy the customers. To help her achieve this she needs to ensure that the tables are set and the room looks welcoming.

The main focus should be on the customer, while Jane has set the task of setting the tables as her priority.

This is not unusual. You probably meet similar situations every day as a customer.

- You go into a shop and wait at the counter while the sales assistants chat together in a corner.
- You go into a bank at lunchtime, the only time you have available, and find a huge queue with only two windows open, because the bank staff are . . . at lunch.
- Banks used to close on Saturday mornings. As they all closed, the customer had no choice but to accept it, despite the fact that it was very inconvenient.
- You book your car into a garage for repairs and are requested to leave it there all day, despite the fact that it may only take a half an hour to complete the job.
- You wait for someone to arrive at your home to repair the central heating. They may arrive at 9 a.m. or at 6 p.m. or at any time in between. You may take a day off work and no one arrives at all!
- You go to hospital for an appointment and you sit on an old bench with no backrest. You find yourself in a queue of twenty people who have all been given the same appointment time of 9 a.m. You are still waiting at 3 o'clock.
- You get into a taxi and the driver insists on playing loud music, much to your annoyance.

The one factor that all of these situations have in common is that they operate to suit the convenience of the organization rather than the customer.

Such instances can be seen as symptoms of an organization putting its own comfort before that of its customers. Often this permeates right through the organization, and can be seen not only in the way they operate but also in the way they market their products.

Such organizations can be said to be **product led** rather than **customer driven**.

THINK POINT

Describe any symptoms of product-led behaviour in your organization.

In order to look at this concept more closely we need to consider some definitions. We need first to look at marketing.

MARKETING

Although there are no management standards which relate specifically to marketing, it is essential for a supervisor to understand some of the basic principles.

Marketing may be thought of as 'satisfying customers' needs at a profit.'

This definition is aimed at those companies which need to make profits, but there are many for whom profit is not the main objective – charities or government departments, for example. Their main objectives may therefore be to stay in business, and for those we could modify the definition to 'continuing to satisfy customers' needs'.

In either case the customer figures as the reason for the organization to exist at all. If we accept these definitions, then the customer will be the main focus of all our efforts. In the United Kingdom, this is a fairly recent concept. In the past, companies simply had what they thought was a good idea for a product, made it and then tried to sell it.

A fine example of this would be the Sinclair C5 electric car, which was no doubt a brilliant invention, but it came about because the company wanted to make it rather than as a result of any indication that there were customers who might want to buy it.

Aiming to be customer driven should not be considered to apply only to companies who are seeking to make profits. John Major's Citizens' Charter (1992) is an acknowledgement that government bodies must take more account of how ordinary people – i.e., their customers – view the services they provide.

Charities too, in a world in which there is ever-growing competition for donations, must recognize that they need to respond to the wishes of potential donors. The Worldwide Fund for Nature is currently introducing a system which will allow donors to choose which project they wish to support and confirm that the money was indeed spent on that project.

Now let's have a look at some other elements of marketing:

- Market research
- Market segmentation
- Positioning
- Branding
- The marketing mix

Let's begin with market research.

MARKET RESEARCH

It's all very well saying that it's necessary to respond to the needs of the customer, but how do we know what they want?

Market research is a systematic method of obtaining information about customers and their requirements. There are two main types.

Primary information comes from research carried out for a specific purpose. A tasting exercise carried out by a confectionery company to find out whether customers preferred milk or plain chocolate would be an example.

Secondary information is the result of analysis of information which is already available, such as an analysis of the number of first-class air tickets sold between London and New York.

MARKET SEGMENTATION

It is important to realize that there are few products today which will be attractive to everyone. Different people have different preferences. This is referred to as market segmentation. A good example of this can be found in a travel agents. If you browse through the shelves you can find a huge variety of holidays aimed at very different types of people:

- 18 to 30 age group
- Senior citizens
- Empty nesters (people whose children have grown up and left home and who find themselves with an increased disposable income)
- Couples
- Independent travellers
- Beach lovers
- People interested in national heritage

POSITIONING

Each brochure you pick up is likely to be aimed at a different segment of the market. So it is vital that the organization is aware of who is likely to find the product appealing. Targeting a product at a particular market segment is known as positioning. If a product is aimed at an inappropriate segment it is unlikely to be successful. The 18 to 30 age group, for example, are unlikely to be happy with a holiday aimed at the senior citizen, while the latter are unlikely to be tempted to attend a 'heavy metal' rock concert.

BRANDING

Branding can be thought of very simply as 'giving a product a name'. The customer learns to associate a number of features with the particular branded product. Branding is becoming increasingly important because it is possible to build up a considerable amount of customer loyalty to a particular brand. This is clearly demonstrated by the popularity throughout the world of chocolate bars like Mars and Kit Kat. Branding can be so powerful that major problems can be encountered if, for any reason, a company needs to change a brand name. Customers do not recognize the new name and cease to buy the product. A considerable amount of investment in promotion and advertising may be necessary to establish the new name. An example of this was the change of Marathon chocolate bar to Snickers, which seems to have been successful.

THE MARKETING MIX

One of the best and most usual ways to understand the principles of marketing is to look at it through the 'marketing mix':

1 Product
2 Price
3 Place
4 Promotion

The marketing mix is often referred to as 'the Four Ps'. We need to look at each of the ingredients in turn.

1 Product

It is important that an organization has information about the type of product that the customer needs before the product is designed. For example, cars are made in many different shapes and sizes to suit the different types of customer at which they are aimed. Great care is taken to research exactly what is required and what features will make them more desirable than those made by competitors. Quality is often a very important issue, and is one that we will be returning to in more detail later.

2 Price

The price which is charged for a product depends upon a number of factors. Obviously it is important that the price is greater than the cost or there will be no profit. For non-profit-making organizations the price needs at least to equal the cost. However, there is not necessarily a direct relationship between cost and price, because the price should reflect what the customer is prepared to pay for the product. Cost savings may allow a reduced price in order to gain a competitive edge, or they may simply mean greater profits.

Profit targets will also affect the price of the product, since people with a financial interest in the company expect a return on their investment.

The price charged by competitors will also have a great bearing on the price a company asks for its products, but it is not always necessary to be the cheapest. Many organizations seek to gain an advantage in quality, which means that their prices may be a little higher than their competitors' but the customer is often prepared to pay a little extra for the benefits that high quality brings. Marks and Spencer is an example of a company which feels that quality is the prime requirement for its customers.

3 Place

Place includes where the product is sold and through what channels. For example, a manufacturer of nuts and bolts might deliver its products directly to the customer's factory, so the customer simply awaits their arrival. On the other hand, products are not always taken direct to the customer. The manufacturer may distribute to a number of warehouses to which the customer may have to go to buy them. This applies in the case of any supermarket or shop.

A football match is another example where the method of distribution involves the customer going to the product. Indeed, in cup competitions, smaller clubs often elect to play at their opponent's ground because of the larger capacity of their stadium. In addition, the football club must decide upon the best day to play the match in order to ensure that the largest possible attendance is gained. So the timing of distribution is just as important as the method of distribution. This can also be demonstrated by large supermarkets opening late before bank holidays. Indeed, many even open on bank holidays now. The corner shop, on the other hand, may have to open early and late every day to offer an extra feature to offset competition by the larger stores.

4 Promotion

Promotion includes all those activities which help to attract a buyer for the product and include:

- advertising
- face-to-face selling
- telephone selling
- special promotions
- public relations
- sponsorship

It is also very important that there is regular liaison with major customers.

All the elements of the marketing mix are interlinked. If one is changed it will have an effect on the other. For example, if the channel of distribution is changed, then promotion may need to be changed too. Alterations to the quality of the product will have an effect on the price and possibly on the amount of money available for promotion.

Philip Kotler (*Marketing Business*, December–January 91/92) considers that by referring to the Four Ps we are still looking at marketing through the eyes of the organization. If we really want to look at it through the eyes of the customer the marketing mix should be the Four Cs:

1 Customer value
2 Cost
3 Communication
4 Convenience

1 Customer value (product): the customer is seeking value for money. On a weekly shopping trip, for example, a customer may decide to buy four oranges costing a pound rather than a pound of apples at eighty-five pence. He or she is prepared to spend an extra fifteen pence because they view the oranges as good value but the apples as overpriced.

2 Cost to the customer (price): apart from the price of an item, the customer is involved in other costs including transport to the point of purchase and the use of their time. Customers may decide to buy clothes from a direct mail catalogue because the overall cost to them may be less than going into town to buy them.

3 Communication (promotion): The customer wants a two-way process in which she or he feels that their needs are being catered for and their voice is being heard.

4 Convenience (place): customers may simply not have time available at certain points of the day. They may need shops to be open late at night or early in the morning. Or they may prefer to shop at an out of town supermarket where parking is easy rather than search for a parking space in town and then have to carry their purchases some distance to the car.

This is actually a good starting point from which to look at Operations.

OPERATIONS

A nice simple definition of operations is

> doing things that your customers want, at an acceptable cost to
> the organization

We can now formulate an operations mix by combining the various
elements of the Four Ps and the Four Cs. The operations mix will be a
combination of one P and three Cs, and look something like this:

- Product
- Cost
- Convenience of purchase
- Customer service

So if, in our operations, we offer a *product* of good value at low *cost*
that is *convenient* for the customer to buy and at the same time we
keep a regular *contact* with our customers and their needs it is likely
that we will satisfy both the customer and the organization. We will
be looking at the various aspects of operations in more detail in later
chapters.

Up to now we have referred only to products. Many people think of
products as tangible things that are manufactured and which you can
see and touch. Yet many of the examples we have looked at so far, and
indeed the case study itself, are concerned with services. In fact the
two are considered by many to be interchangeable: services are
simply the products of service industries. A number of differences are
sometimes put forward, such as:

- Services involve the customer during the operations process.
  For example, a hairdresser needs a customer to be present
  when giving a haircut. However, the customer is often closely
  involved with a manufactured product, especially during the
  design stage. For example, airlines often work very closely
  with aeroplane manufacturers to ensure that the design meets
  the specific requirements of the company.
- Services are perishable. For example, when an aeroplane
  leaves an airport, any seats not sold are completely wasted
  and can earn no money for the airline. However, many manu-

factured products are perishable in the same way. All dairy products have limited shelf lives while products like cooked meats or sausages must be sold very quickly.

- People who provide a service are part of the service itself. However, most customers buying products identify everyone involved with the company as part of the product. If you were the manager of a factory buying machine tools, your view of the products would be influenced if the staff of the supplier were always rude or ill-dressed.

So it is often difficult to differentiate between product and service. Many activities involve both. For example, a supermarket provides a service by selling own-labelled goods which have been manufactured. Similarly, a light engineering firm may have a small shop on the premises where it sells nuts and bolts on a retail basis.

Throughout this book, therefore, we will use the word 'product' to mean either manufactured product or service product.

THINK POINT

Analyse your own organization. Do you provide services or manufacture products, or both?

Now we can have a look at some of the relationships that we will find when analysing the operations function.

OPERATIONS AND OPERATIONS DEPARTMENTS

A distinction needs to be made here between operations and the Operations Department. Everyone is involved in operations every day just by going to work and doing their job. In the latter case your customers are other people within the organization, that is, internal customers.

INTERNAL CUSTOMERS

Whether you are in the finance, personnel, marketing or any other department, whatever you are doing can be classed as operations because you are satisfying the definition of operations that we looked at earlier ('doing things for your customers at an acceptable cost to the organization').

In finance, for example, you will be providing a service to other departments, who will be your internal customers. Internal customers should be viewed in the same way as external customers. They are, after all, the reason why your department is in business. Without them you would have nothing to do.

The operations department, on the other hand, has a specialized role concerning actual production of the *end* product usually (but not always) for the external customer.

THINK POINT

Consider your own department.
• Who are your customers?
• Can you identify both internal and external customers?

RELATIONSHIPS BETWEEN DEPARTMENTS

It is important to look at the relationship between the Operations Department and the other departments in an organization.

A typical company may look like that shown in figure 1.1.

The marketing department will find out

• what the customer needs
• when it needs to be available
• the price that is likely to be acceptable

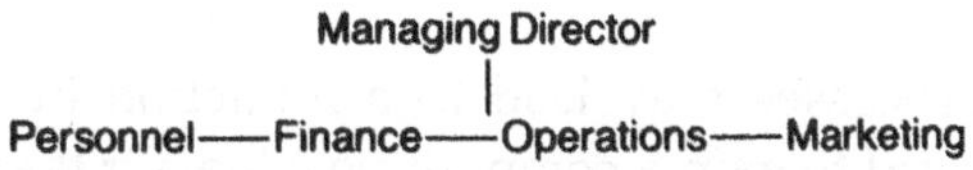

Managing Director
|
Personnel——Finance——Operations——Marketing

Figure 1.1 A typical company hierarchy

The operations department can then be given definite targets concerning

- the products to be made
- product quality
- costs
- delivery schedules

The personnel department provides a service to other departments, including giving advice on

- training
- conditions of service
- rates of pay
- manpower planning
- recruitment and selection of staff

The finance department will give a continual service concerning

- apportioning of costs
- budgets
- performance

MARKETING AND OPERATIONS

The relationship between the marketing and operations departments must be a very close one. It is too simplistic to say that the operations department produces what the marketing department tells it to, but certainly the marketing department should be in the lead.

Having said that, the operations department is often the place that feedback is received from the customer, and we will look at this in much more detail in a later chapter.

Further, there are many instances of innovations by the operations department, usually the 'research and development' function, inventing new processes or even new products which allow marketing initiatives to be made. An example would be new technology in banks, such as the introduction of debit cards for ease of use instead of cheques.

Often, new processes may lead to a reduction in costs, allowing prices to be reduced to gain a competitive edge. Or they may allow an increase in quality. This is certainly the case with many Japanese companies, especially the automobile manufacturers. The continual improvements in their operating processes have allowed costs to be reduced and quality to be improved, with the result that high quality products are sold at very competitive prices.

The most important point is that there should be a match between what the marketing function want for the customer and what the operations function can provide. If the customer is promised too much and the organization is unable to deliver, this leads to disappointment. It is much better to take a more realistic view and not to commit the organization to something it is not able to do.

To illustrate the effect on customers of failing to meet expectations, we might consider the railway industry. In the UK, for a variety of reasons, British Rail run a consistently high-speed Inter City service. Consequently, the advertised journey times between major cities is impressively short. If a train is fifteen minutes late on a three-hour journey, passengers complain about the terrible service and murmurs of 'British Rail late again' are heard.

A similar journey in Germany, for example, might be advertised at three and a half hours, but the train arrives on time. The passengers praise the efficiency of the service and say how wonderful it is. Yet if we analyse the two, we find that the British Rail train has taken three hours and fifteen minutes and caused dissatisfaction, while the German train has taken three and a half hours and everyone is delighted.

The important point here is that in the case of the BR train, excellent though the performance was, it did not live up to expectations and the customers were disappointed.

If we go back to our case study, the customers who left the hotel had very high expectations from reading about it in the brochure.

So promising more than an organization can deliver will inevitably lead to customer dissatisfaction.

We referred earlier to a new system being brought in at the Worldwide Fund for Nature in order to provide information to donors. The system is also intended to allow the fundraising (marketing) and projects (operations) departments to work much more closely together. Project managers will be able to see where funds are likely to come from for their projects, and will be able to identify any shortfalls so that fundraisers can seek more funds for that particular project.

THE ENVIRONMENT

The environment within which organizations operate has a very great influence on what the organization does. In fact there are two kinds of environment: external and internal.

THE EXTERNAL ENVIRONMENT

The external environment is made up of those factors which have an impact on the organization but are outside its control. They can be divided into four main areas:

- Political
- Economic
- Sociological
- Technological

Not surprisingly, an examination of these areas is referred to as a PEST analysis.

Political factors

Examples would include:

- European Community decisions such as the maximum 48-hour week
- Political regulation of industry
- Statutory incomes policies
- Widening the scope of VAT

Economic factors

Examples include:

- Exchange rates
- Interest rates
- Boom/recession

Social factors

Examples include:

- The trend towards greater affluence leading to increased demand for luxury products
- The trend towards longer lifespan which means that people have more time to enjoy their retirement
- The trend towards environmentally friendly products
- Cultural differences between countries

Technological factors

Examples include:

- New information systems
- More powerful and economical engines
- Miniaturization (such as computers)
- Mobility (telephones)
- New communication systems (video conferencing)

The external environment is constantly changing and organizations need to adapt continually in order to keep pace with it. They do this by carrying out a PEST analysis, as discussed above.

Organizations which do not monitor trends and changes in their environment are often overtaken by events. It is not enough simply to react once a change has occurred because it may be too late.

For example, if the birth rate fell in a particular year you can reasonably assume that ten years on there may be fewer ten-year-olds than before. If you are manufacturing children's toys, for example, you would need to be aware of such trends.

OTWS (Otherwise) analysis (also known as SWOT analysis)

You can remember this by thinking, 'Organizations must carry out this analysis *Otherwise* they may go out of business.

OTWS (Otherwise) stands for:

Opportunities
Threats } which concern the external environment

Weaknesses
Strengths } which concern the internal environment

From the PEST analysis it is possible to identify opportunities and threats in the external environment.

The fact that people are generally more affluent has meant that there are many opportunities in the travel industry, since many people now take more than one holiday. Saga Holidays have built up their business through the fact that senior citizens now tend to be both healthier and wealthier than before.

On the other hand, Harrods realized that British people were turning away from real fur coats. To meet this threat, they recently stopped selling them and turned to synthetic substitutes. There are, however, cultural differences in different countries. Furs are still very popular in Italy and, as you might expect, in Scandinavian countries.

Some factors are both threats and opportunities.

Long playing record sales have been dropping for some time due to competition from new forms of technology such as cassettes and compact discs. It seems likely that they will disappear altogether from most record shops. However, some enterprising companies may find a niche specializing in selling LPs to enthusiasts who still want to buy them.

We have looked at the external environment, but as we mentioned before, there is also the internal environment.

INTERNAL ENVIRONMENT

The internal environment is made up of what happens within the organization itself. In order to analyse it we need to examine the organization's strengths and weaknesses.

Strengths would include such factors as

- Reputation
- Dedicated staff
- New equipment
- Strong management team
- Strong financial position
- Loyal shareholders
- Good training schemes

Weaknesses would of course include the opposite of these, but might also be represented by:

- Quality problems
- Low share price
- Policy disagreements
- Poor cash flow
- Poor credit ratings

Having analysed the strengths and weaknesses internally, we can then match them up to the external opportunities and threats by using the OTWS analysis, in which we identify what strengths the organization can build upon and the weaknesses it needs to minimize in order to take advantage of the opportunities or avert the threats.

Case Note 2

Elaine Benton is sitting at her desk in the hotel. She is the catering supervisor.

She is responsible for all catering arrangements in the hotel. This is a rather large responsibility since there are two bars, a coffee lounge, a restaurant, a banqueting room for conferences and weddings, while the leisure complex has a poolside bar which also offers lunches and light snacks.

Elaine can see problems looming ahead. First, and most serious, a new restaurant is due to open only fifty yards down the road. She has heard that they have secured the services of a well-known chef, with a reputation for producing the finest French food. To make matters worse, a recent review in the local newspaper referred to her own restaurant as being of very good quality but rather unadventurous.

In addition, Friday nights in the bar were very popular with young people. This was mainly because they went to a disco across the road which opened at ten o'clock in the evening and they met in the bar for a couple of hours, moving on at about ten thirty. They were a very well behaved crowd and there had never been any trouble. However, the disco had only had a lease for two years and would close in three weeks time – the premises would be turned into offices. There were no other discos nearby and the closest one was four miles away. Clearly there was a likelihood that this particular trade would be lost.

Finally, the recession meant that business as a whole for the hotel was down on the previous year, with fewer people coming to stay.

This had a knock-on effect on the restaurants and bars, which were showing a corresponding decrease on last year. Incidents like those last week didn't help. She had been on her way towards the coffee lounge when she saw a couple stride out, clearly irritated, a fact emphasized by the way that the woman threw a brochure into the waste bin as she left. It was too late for her to do anything, but she had spoken to Jane about it. Jane did her best and worked hard, but she really hadn't been given much training since she joined the staff. Come to think of it, neither had the others. She would have to give that some thought.

On the bright side, however, the new leisure complex was booming due to the fact that more and more people were seeking to look after their health by taking exercise and keeping fit. Sales of light snacks and mineral water were double what they were last year.

Elaine smiled wryly, 'Yes, a bright spot on a bleak horizon'.

Elaine needs to do an OTWS analysis.

THINK POINT

Can you carry out an OTWS analysis for her?

Opportunities:

- In the area of health and fitness
- More local trade

Threats:

- The new restaurant opening soon
- The recession
- The disco due to close

Strengths:

- Good leisure complex
- Reputation for quality

- A large range of facilities in the hotel
- Popular with young people
- Hard working staff
- People staying overnight use the hotel facilities

Weaknesses:

- Unadventurous restaurant
- Relying on another business for trade on Fridays
- Trade relies on people staying rather than being locally based
- Not much training for staff

Having completed her OTWS analysis, Elaine can consider some strategies.

Case Note 3

Elaine pondered for a while and then began to smile. Things were never as bad as they seemed. The new restaurant would be a threat, of course, but they would probably aim at local trade. With their reputation for quality, most people staying at the hotel would probably continue to eat there, especially if the menu were to be improved and perhaps made more adventurous. There might be a spin-off here for the hotel, if the advertising and promotion by the new restaurant owners were to increase general interest and awareness among local people in eating out. Clearly, the owners of the new restaurant felt that there was a market among local people, so why shouldn't the hotel try to win some of it?

This year's results had clearly shown that the hotel restaurant was relying too much on guests who were staying, so it was essential that an effort be made to increase local trade. Perhaps this new threat could be turned into an opportunity!

On the other hand, there was clearly a weakness in the lack of training for staff – for example, Jane and the others. In addition, if the menu was to be made more adventurous, could she just assume that Marc, the chef, would be able to cope? He had been doing the same things for years now.

There was also the fact that they had never really advertised much locally. They appeared more in brochures than in the local newspapers. How could they attract more local customers?

She turned her thoughts to the disco that would soon be closed.

She thought about the fact that the hotel relied upon it for the Friday trade and would not be able to do so in the future. It would have to rely on itself. Well, there were enough rooms in the hotel: the banqueting room, for example, was enormous and had hardly ever been used since it was introduced. Why couldn't they put on their own attraction, not only retaining their customers but keeping them after 10:30 too?

Then there was the leisure complex. People were becoming more and more health conscious. The light snacks served there were all made from healthy ingredients, and many of the dishes were vegetarian. They had a couple of very good suppliers whose products were of the highest quality. Perhaps the health factor could be extended to the main restaurant and incorporated with the new menus? She would talk to Marc.

Elaine was elated. She had started off being very gloomy about the threats to the business. Now she realized that they could all be turned into opportunities. There would be no stopping them now!

In the case study we saw that our hotel actually has several different facilities:

- The bars
- The coffee lounge
- Guest rooms
- The restaurant
- The banqueting room
- The leisure centre

We can refer to these as a range of products much in the same way as the manufacturer of tools might have a range of different products, such as hammers, files or chisels.

Each product has a definite life span, which is referred to as the product life cycle.

THE PRODUCT LIFE CYCLE

The stages in the life cycle can be identified as follows:

- Launch
- Growth

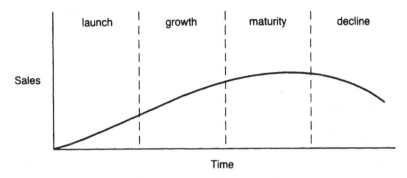

Figure 1.2 The product life cycle

- Maturity
- Decline

The diagram in figure 1.2. illustrates the different stages.

The launch stage is concerned with establishing the new product and creating awareness among potential customers. It is likely to need a lot of investment, in money and effort, and at this stage is likely to produce little profit. Many products progress no further than this stage.

There follows a period of rapid growth as the idea catches on and customer awareness increases. The product will be distributed ever more widely and customer loyalty will begin to develop. Competitors may begin to enter the market. Profits may begin to rise rapidly.

During the mature stage, competition will increase and sales and profits will level out. It is in the interests of the organization that this stage should last as long as possible.

Due to any of a number of factors, such as increasing competition, obsolescence of the product or changing customer preferences, there comes a time when sales begin to decrease and decisions need to be taken as to whether to try to extend the life of the product or whether to withdraw from it altogether.

The total length of the product cycle and the stages within it differs from product to product. Some products may have a very short life cycle. Programmes sold at the opera or at a football match might only be available for a matter of hours and be of limited value after the event. Cameras are very quickly overtaken by new technology. Some breakfast cereals, on the other hand, seem to go on for years in the mature stage without any sign of the decline stage being reached.

It is possible to extend the life cycle of most products by **modifying** them or aiming them at different types of customers (**repositioning**).

MODIFICATION

When the sales of a particular product begin to fall off and it is clear that the decline stage is approaching, it is possible to change the product in some way to make it more attractive and thus prolong its life. New versions of the same basic product with the addition of special features are continually being produced. The Boeing 747 has been around for a long time, but is continually updated to take account of new technology and changing customer preferences.

REPOSITIONING

In our earlier example, a commemorative programme for an opera may be of little use to many people afterwards but might be of great value to a limited number of collectors long after the event. So, before the event, the programme would be aimed (positioning) at those attending. Afterwards, it might be aimed at collectors in an attempt to increase the life cycle. This is known as **repositioning.**

A good example of repositioning can be found among Johnson's Baby Products. The reduction in the birth rate was clearly a threat to future sales of baby soap and talcum powder. Recently, the company has turned its attention to adults by stressing how good such gentle products will be for their skin.

Similarly, Lucozade used to be considered as a drink for people who were feeling a little off colour or who were recovering from illness. No longer! Adverts now show young sportsmen in the prime of life drinking it to replace the energy they have just used up. The product has been repositioned to appeal to the fit and healthy too.

THINK POINT

Consider the hotel in the case study. Try to identify which stage in the life cycle the various products have reached.

The bars and coffee lounge are probably in the mature stage, as they have been operating for some time. However, the fact that business activity is down on the previous year because of the recession, indicates that there may be signs that the decline stage is being reached. The same applies to the guest rooms.

The restaurant is also in the mature stage and is facing the imminent prospect of increased competition, which could mark the beginning of the decline stage. However, Elaine feels that they have relied too much on the guests staying at the hotel and they should now be concentrating more on attracting local custom. This is a repositioning of the product which should help to prolong the mature stage.

The banqueting room has never been used much and has not really emerged from the launch stage. Again, Elaine has some thoughts about using it to attract the young people when their disco closes. The leisure centre is clearly in the growth stage and there are high hopes of long-lasting success.

THE BOSTON CONSULTING GROUP MATRIX

Because products have a definite life cycle, most organizations have a portfolio of products, so that as one approaches the decline stage another is in the process of being developed to take its place. The Boston Consulting Group Matrix (see figure 1.3) allows us to look at the product portfolio in relation to: the growth rate of the market; and the market share.

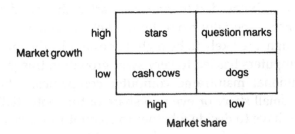

Figure 1.3 The Boston Consulting Group Matrix

Cash cows

These are products which have reached the mature stage in their product life cycle, are producing regular profits, and might be used to develop stars. The market is fairly static and the product has a high market share. Mars Bars or Kit Kats are good examples.

Stars

These are products which have a high market share of a fast-growing market. They may need a lot of investment to ensure success against the strong competition that may be attracted, but are likely to be the cash cows of the future. In the late seventies, the haulage group TNT introduced a premium parcel delivery service which guaranteed delivery the next morning. It gained a high share of a very fast growing market. Today TNT premium service would be regarded as a cash cow.

Dogs

With a low share of a static market dogs are the least attractive in the product portfolio. They may well be sold off or discontinued altogether. With the decline of the traditional heavy industries such as coal and steel, British Rail finds its bulk distribution company, Railfreight, in the position of having a low share of an ever decreasing market.

Question marks

The problem here is in deciding whether to proceed. The market is growing rapidly but the product has a low market share. Considerable investment may be needed to increase market share and competition will be intense, especially from the market leaders. The rewards for success, though, are likely to be high. For example, the introduction of personal computers has led to very swift growth in this market. Some of the traditional mainframe computer companies, who currently have a very small share or even no share of this potentially lucrative market, may have to decide whether to commit resources to compete for this business or to leave it to the market leaders and miss out on a possible opportunity.

Most organizations, then, will have a portfolio of products which will allow them to take into account the need to have a product in the development stage ready for the time when others come to the end of their life cycle. They can also use the profits from cash cows to invest in the products of the future.

> **THINK POINT**
>
> Using either the product life cycle or the Boston Matrix, try to analyse the product portfolio of your organization.

SUMMARY

Supervisory Management Standards:

Unit 1   Maintain services and operations to meet quality standards
Element 1.1 Maintain services and operations
Unit 2   Contribute to the planning, monitoring and control of resources
Element 2.1 Plan for the use of resources
Unit 5   Contribute to the planning, organization and evaluation of work
Element 5.1 Contribute to planning work activities and methods to achieve objectives

To be successful an organization should focus on the customer.

It is important to understand the marketing strategy of your organization.

The marketing and operations functions should work together very closely to achieve a match between what the customer requires and what the organization is capable of producing.

Customers may be internal or external.

The external environment in which an organization exists is constantly changing. It is necessary, therefore, to monitor it continuously to ensure that any opportunities may be developed and potential threats foreseen. It is essential that the internal environment responds to meet these changes. PEST and Otherwise analysis are very helpful in this respect.

Products have a definite life cycle, though the length of the cycle differs according to the product.

Many organizations have a variety of products to ensure that they are constantly developing new ones to replace those that are in decline.

Chapter 2

The Operations Process

Supervisory Management Standards:

Unit 1   Maintain services and operations to meet quality
              standards
Element 2.1 Plan for the use of resources

Let's return to our definition of operations as 'doing things that your customers want at an acceptable cost to the organization'. What does this involve? In its simplest form it means turning effort and resources into something that the customer wants. A model would look like that illustrated in figure 2.1. We shall explore the elements of the model in greater detail.

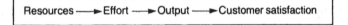

Resources ⟶ Effort ⟶ Output ⟶ Customer satisfaction

Figure 2.1 An operations model

RESOURCES

- Basic raw materials such as sand for making concrete
- Materials which have already been made by another process, such as a fuel pump for a car engine
- Fixed machinery which will be used to convert the materials into the finished products
- People, who will use the machinery or be directly involved in providing a service
- Skills to enable people to perform to the best of their ability

- Ideas to provide innovation and lead to new technology
- Finance to ensure that money is available as required

Effort

Effort involves using the resources to produce a new end product. Wild (1985) identified four types of transformation process. These have been expanded by the authors into five basic methods below:

1 Physical change
2 Assembly
3 Change of ownership
4 Change of place
5 Change of state of the customer

1 The *physical change* of the raw materials into finished products. Thus iron ore is combined with various other materials to make steel, while a number of chemicals might be changed into fertilizer. The manufacture of plastics would also fall into this category.

2 The *assembly* of finished products to make up a new product. This is most obvious in the motor car industry, in which various parts might be made in different places and by different manufacturers, and then are brought together in one factory for final assembly.

3 A change in *ownership* takes place in shops and supermarkets. There is often a series of transactions involving importer, wholesaler, shop, customer; and a change of ownership may occur at each stage.

4 A change of *place* occurs in the transport and distribution industries. Manufactured goods are delivered as freight, while people are moved around as passengers. The Post Office is a major player in the distribution industry, delivering millions of letters per day. Transport of freight very often involves a change of ownership too. It is vital that the exact point at which this occurs is established by all the parties involved. For example, goods in the process of being transported may belong to:

- The sender (known as the consignor), as is usually the case when you send a parcel by one of the many carriers available
- The transport company, as is sometimes the case in shipping,

when the shipping company itself may purchase the cargo, transport it and resell it at destination

- The person who is to receive them (consignee), which is often the case in direct mail services when the customer is often charged insurance to cover against the package being lost in transit
- An agent or other third party may own the goods, as in shipping when the goods may be owned by neither consignor, transporters nor consignee

A written contract is usual in order to specify the exact terms upon which an item is carried so that in the event of a mishap it is clear to whom the goods belong.

5 A change in the *state of the customer* is most usual in service industries. A customer leaves a pub or restaurant feeling better, it is hoped, than he or she went in. Similarly, a customer's appearance will be altered by a visit to a hairdresser, while someone might feel uplifted after giving a donation to charity.

Many organizations are involved in more than one of these processes. For example, a baker who makes his own bread and cakes is involved in transforming the raw materials, and then transfers the ownership to his customers who, especially if it is a fresh cream cake, may experience a change in state: elation in most cases, or guilt if they are supposed to be on a diet!

A restaurant is involved in four of the processes. It will transform raw materials into main courses. Salads will be made by assembling different vegetables that have already been prepared. Wine will be bought from a wholesaler and then sold to the customers, who will leave the restaurant feeling much happier than when they entered.

An airline will be involved in all of these processes as it will:

- transform the place of its passengers
- change raw food into cooked meals
- assemble the various meals into packs to allow the appropriate menus to be taken on board
- change the state of the customer by flying them to their holiday destinations

---

THINK POINT

Which transformation processes occur in your organization?

OUTPUTS

Finished products, including manufactured goods or services which have reached the desired quality, should lead directly to customer satisfaction. They may then form the resources stage of another operations cycle, either within the same organization, if the customer was internal, or in another organization if the customer was external.

For example, the finished nut or bolt may be used in the next stage of the manufacturing process within a company which manufactures machine tools, or may be sold to another company and used as part of their resources in the manufacture of another product.

Rejected items, such as nuts and bolts of incorrect dimensions, which have failed the quality standards laid down but have been detected before reaching the customer, may be returned to the input stage of the process for further work to be done or sold to a company which uses scrap metal as a resource in its operations cycle.

Waste products, including substances which are hazardous to the environment (such as oils and chemicals), will become the raw material for specialist organizations who deal in their safe removal. Used paper in government organizations is sold to companies which recycle it. Scrap metal is used in the production of steel.

Profits are an expected output. During the *effort* stage (see figure 2.1 at the beginning of this chapter) value is added to all the resources that have been put in so that the value of the outputs exceeds the value of the resources used. Profits are one of the main sources of finance used by companies in their investment pro-grammes. They will be looked at in greater detail in volume three of *In Charge: Managing Finance and Information*.

The outputs we have considered so far all either lead to customer satisfaction or at least avoid customer dissatisfaction. They are part of a continual cycle of operations models in which the finished products of one process form the resources that are used in the next process.

However, finished products which have not reached the desired quality and have not been detected before reaching the customer will lead to dissatisfaction. Cars with faults are an obvious example in manufacturing, but there are many instances in supermarkets of items being past their sell-by dates or of bread being stale. We will be looking at quality in chapter 5.

We have looked at the operations model in detail, and it now looks like that illustrated in figure 2.2. Most products or services can be considered as forming part of the input process of another operating system. Even those which at first you think might not be, are often, on further inspection, found to qualify.

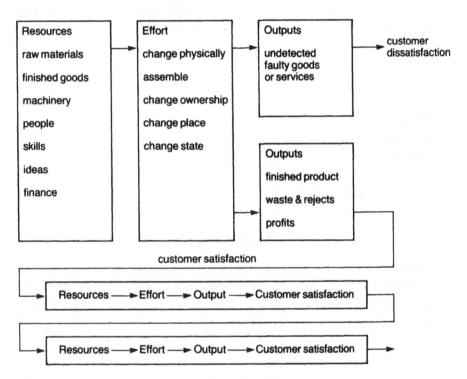

Figure 2.2 A continual operations model

For example, if you eat a chocolate bar, the waste wrapper becomes a part of the input process for refuse collectors. A person recovering from a hospital operation may become an input into the physiotherapy department. Someone who has just had a slap-up meal in a restaurant may well need a taxi home!

THINK POINT

Can you identify the various outputs of your organization? Do they form part of the inputs for another operating process?

Before we look in more detail at the actual planning and organizing of work it may be useful to consider the different types of operating systems that you may find in your organization. There are five main types:

1 Jobbing
2 Batch
3 Line
4 Continuous
5 Project

Let's look at each in turn.

1 Jobbing

Jobbing involves tailoring a service or product to a particular customer's requirements. In fact bespoke tailoring is itself a good example of this because each suit is made to measure for a particular customer. Landscape gardeners and cabinet makers are other good examples.

2 Batch

Organizations which use a batch process will produce a number of the same items or services over a period of time. The same machines or systems will then be reset to produce another batch of a different product, or a similar product of different size or style. Some organizations produce batches of different parts of the product at the same time and then use another batch process to assemble them.

The fashion industry is a good example. Machines will be set to produce a number of a particular garment. When the required number have been made they will then be used to make another style or size.

In a bakery, bread will be baked in one batch, then the oven will be adjusted to allow cakes to be processed. Pies will be made up of separate batches of filling and pastry, possibly at the same time by different people. They will then be combined and cooked in the oven in another batch (see figure 2.3).

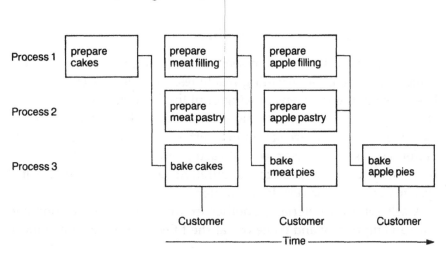

Figure 2.3 A simplified diagram of a batch process in a bakery

Process 1 makes up a batch of meat pie filling, then concentrates on making apple pie filling in the next batch. Process 2 makes up a batch of meat pie pastry and then turns to making sweeter apple pie pastry. In process 3 a batch of cakes, which have been prepared previously in process 1, are baked and then made available to the customer.

Next into the oven is the combined meat filling and pastry produced by processes 1 and 2. When ready they too are made available to the customer. The apple pies follow the meat pies in the next batch.

A local authority will send out all of the demands for payment of the Council Tax in one run. The computer system will then be set up again to produce other invoices (or reminders for the original bill).

An engineering firm will run off one order of tools or fasteners of a particular specification, before changing the settings of the machines for the next. Or it may produce batches of different parts on separate machines and then assemble them in another batch.

Because of the need continually to reset machines and systems, batch is a complicated process which requires a great deal of planning and communication if it is to be carried out effectively.

Its main advantages are that:

- the same equipment can be used to produce a variety of products in the required volumes
- it is a flexible system which allows different parts of an organization to work on separate parts of the product ready for final assembly or combination

3 Line

The line process is most often seen in manufacturing of cars or consumer goods, such as washing machines. Parts are assembled on a line which in theory keeps moving until the finished product appears at the end. The line process differs from batch in that a number of machines or systems are set up in a certain way, for a long period, to perform one step of the process at each point in the line. They are not continually reset to produce a different product. Essentially line systems are used for very long run items.

A self-service cafeteria is another example. You start at one end with an empty tray and come out at the till with a three course meal.

4 Continuous

A continuous system relates to those processes which deal with one product and are totally given over to it, such as oil or chemical pipelines, which flow on a continual basis. They can also be found in the service industry in self-service petrol pumps.

5 Project

A good example of a project is the Channel Tunnel. It requires the very precise control of a variety of different organizations, including government bodies, local planning authorities, architects, construction companies, transport companies, engineers etc. They all need to be brought together in a planned and structured manner to ensure that deadlines are met, quality is maintained and costs are controlled.

Projects may be as complex as the Tunnel or a large budget film, or they may be more simple, such as planning a wedding reception or even arranging to buy and sell houses. What they have in common is that they require the coordination of a number of operations, some of which will go on at the same time, while others will depend upon the completion of other operations before they can begin.

Buying a house often depends upon the sale of the house you

already have being completed before you commit yourself to the new one (or even more likely you will arrange a simultaneous completion). You are also unlikely to sign on the dotted line before your solicitor has been satisfied that everything is in order.

We will look at some techniques to assist in planning projects in the next chapter.

Meanwhile let's take another visit to our hotel.

Case Note 4

Marc, the chef, looked out of the window of the large kitchen. He had a lot on his mind. Apart from the usual events of the day, a private function was being held that evening in the banqueting room. He had met the organizer of the function a couple of weeks ago and had agreed a very interesting menu with her, including a couple of alternatives to give people a choice and to cater for vegetarians.

He had made all of the dishes before at the hotel, so he had no worries about his ability to provide them.

The organizer had taken the guests' orders and had supplied Marc with an exact written specification, so he was quite clear as to what was required.

There were twenty dinner guests altogether. Twenty was not a difficult number to cater for and he had liaised with Elaine to ensure that there would be sufficient staff available. She had confirmed that there would be four waiters/waitresses on duty and that the head waiter would look in from time to time. The dinner was scheduled for 7:30 and it was expected that people would begin to arrive from 7 o'clock. The head waiter would greet them as they arrived. He had been given a guest list and a seating plan.

He looked at the list of the required dishes which is reproduced below.

Starters	
Prawn cocktail	14
Melon Surprise	4
Bayonne Ham	2
Main Courses	
Roast Leg of Lamb	10
Baked Trout	5
Vegetable Lasagne	5

Vegetables

potatoes	15
carrots	15
peas	15
cauliflower	15
mixed salad for lasagne	5

Sweets

Lemon Pudding	7
Syllabub	7
Fruit Salad	6

Cheese

A mixture of three cheeses would be offered to each guest:

Leicester	20
Stilton	20
Brie	20
Coffee and biscuits	20

He had placed the order with his meat and fish suppliers several days ago, and this would be delivered fresh during the morning before 11 o'clock. We will look in more detail in a later chapter at how the order was made up. He had given James, his assistant, a list in order that he could tick off the contents of the order as it arrived. He had also told him to contact the supplier if it had not arrived by 11:20. James had a superb eye for meat and fish, and Marc knew that he would reject it if it fell below the quality expected. The supplier knew that too so it was unlikely to happen. James had checked with him this morning and Marc had confirmed that he should reject anything that he felt was not up to standard. In that case, James would go into town and buy the meat from another supplier. He had been told how much he could spend overall if this proved necessary. Meanwhile, Marc was off to market to buy the vegetables.

'Before you go Marc, I've just had a thought. Yesterday, there were some excellent pineapples at a good price and they would be great for the fruit salad.'

THINK POINT

Which of the five types of production system has the case study described?

The answer is jobbing, because the service is being tailor-made to suit the client.

Now let's look at how some of the other production systems work in practice.

Case Note 5

It was seven o'clock and people were beginning to drift down to the dining room for breakfast. Jill, the breakfast cook, was just winding up into overdrive. There were eighty guests staying and breakfast was a complicated business. There were four main parts to each breakfast:

- tea/coffee
- cereal/fruit juice
- cooked breakfast
- toast and jam/marmalade

Not only have they to be made up; they also have to be served to the guests. To complicate matters further, breakfast is spread over a period of three hours so people can turn up at any time. Experience has shown, however, that the greatest demand will be from 7:30 to 8:30.

Batch

The tables had been set the night before so the first task for Jane and the other four waiters/waitresses was to lay out fruit juice and cereals on a large, central table for guests to help themselves. Individual butter and sugar dishes were also placed on each table.

As each guest arrived they would be welcomed, asked what they would like to drink during their breakfast and invited to help themselves to juice and cereal. At the same time, their order for breakfast would be taken.

Batch

In the kitchen, Jill was already hard at work. She had made up a row of cafetières with the required amount of ground coffee in them, ready to receive the hot water. A row of individual teapots were also filled ready with teabags.

The hotplates were singing with the sound of sausages and bacon being fried, while sauté potatoes were sizzling away in another pan. Tomatoes and mushrooms were under the grill.

Batch

Jill would cook a steady stream of sausage, bacon, potatoes, mushrooms and tomatoes because most guests would ask for a selection of these. They could also be kept hot for a short while without spoiling or overcooking so she usually prepared six portions at a time. When she had only two portions remaining she would cook another batch. During the busy period, however, she would start on the next batch straight away.

Jobbing/Batch

Toast, on the other hand, was a bit more problematical as it could go tough and leathery as it cooled. She made the toast for each order as it was received, except in the busy period when she produced one batch after another.

Jobbing

The other two main variables were eggs and fish. Guests could have a variety of eggs: scrambled, poached, fried (soft or hard) or boiled. They might want one or two. Eggs therefore had to wait for each order and then be cooked to the individual requirements.

Jobbing

Fish was not particularly popular, and she would only receive one or two orders throughout the whole breakfast period, so they too were made to order.

Jobbing

By 9:00 the majority of the guests finished breakfast, and Jill allowed all of the food to run out and cooked each order as it was received in order to avoid waste.

Batch

The waiters/waitresses who had been involved in a continual cycle of taking orders, serving, clearing away, began to relax.

Line

So far we have not mentioned John, who helped Jill in the kitchen and whose main task was dealing with the dirty dishes as they returned. Until a few years ago, there had been two helpers, one scraped the dishes and washed them, while the other dried and stacked, in a mini production line. Now, most of the production line was taken over by the dishwashing machine, and John's role was to load and empty it and return the dishes to their appropriate place.

By 9:45 everyone was beginning to relax towards the end of another successful breakfast. It was at that moment that the toaster caught fire. It quickly went ablaze, but John was very quick-thinking and immediately picked up the fire extinguisher and put it out in a matter of seconds.

Continuous

That was long enough, however, for the smoke alarm to have been put into operation and the automatic sprinklers that had been newly installed came into operation. Jill and John were soaked, but unharmed. John was very philosophical about it: 'I suppose it's nice to know that the alarm and sprinklers are working every minute of every day to ensure our safety.'

The case note illustrates a number of points about the different types of systems. Clearly, jobbing has advantages in that you use exactly the amount of materials and time to produce what the customer needs, and they receive their eggs exactly the way they want them. There are no economies of scale however, and it is less cost-effective in terms of manpower, cooking time and electricity to cook individually rather than in a batch.

The waiters/waitresses would take a number of orders at once, allowing them to be processed in the kitchen in a batch. They would also clear away dirty dishes in a number of batches, allowing them to be put into the dishwashing machine together. Batch systems do require careful planning for them to operate well, especially in manufacturing industries where there may be a number of interrelated batch operations. Even in our example here we can see how the various operations need to be linked together. For example, if the clearing away of dirty dishes is not linked to the dishwashing cycle, the kitchen could be cluttered up with them, leaving little room to work.

The dishwashing arrangements are a good example of a mini production line, in that the dishes move along from one process to another until they end up being stored away:

- cleared from the tables
- loaded into dishwasher
- washing cycle
- unloaded
- stored away

The fire alarm/sprinkler system is an example of a dedicated system in continuous operation. We will be looking at health and safety matters in chapter 8.

There is one production system that we haven't seen in action yet, so let's look at an example of a project.

Case Note 6

It was one o'clock in the morning and the first Disco to be held in the hotel had just finished.

'What a disaster!'

Elaine surveyed the empty room. It was a mess. Things had gone badly out of control, that much was clear. Now they had to pick up the pieces and decide where to go from here.

We saw from Elaine's, the Catering Supervisor's, PEST and Otherwise analysis that the local disco was closing down and the hotel was likely to lose a good deal of Friday evening's takings. She had come up with the idea of the hotel holding its own disco on Fridays in the banqueting room, thus bringing into operation a seldom used resource and at the same time protecting Fridays' revenue.

She began to analyse what had gone wrong.

It had started off well. She had done some market research by going to the local disco herself during its last few weeks of operation and making notes of what the young people seemed to like.

She had followed this up with a series of personal interviews to find out their reaction to the hotel providing the disco. The response had been very favourable. She had then used the Four Ps to look at the service that should be given.

The product would be a carbon copy of what was being done now, and she would ask the current disco operators simply to transfer their show to the hotel.

The price, she felt, ought to be a little bit cheaper to begin with, to ensure that sufficient people attended.

The place would be the banqueting room. It was very convenient, as the hotel was on all the major bus routes and, in any case, many of the potential customers already spent the evening in the hotel.

Promotion would be tackled in a number of ways:

First, a large notice during the last two weeks of the disco, with the agreement of the current operators, would be displayed at the disco itself.

Further notices would be displayed at the hotel itself.

An advert would be taken out in the local weekly newspaper showing the Grand Opening and offering a number of prizes during the first two weeks. This, together with the slightly cheaper price, ought to do the trick.

So far so good.

Elaine also knew that it was important that the hotel was capable of meeting the specifications that she had set during her marketing exercise. In fact, all along she had consulted the people concerned to try to ensure that everything would go as advertised.

It was not as simple as it seemed at first. There were a number of problems that needed to be overcome before the disco could take place:

- The hotel manager, her boss, would have to be convinced that the whole plan was workable and cost-effective.
- The banqueting room did not have sufficient electrical sockets in the right places to suit the disco operators.
- A stage area would need to be created.
- The whole lighting scheme was completely inappropriate.
- Extra staff would have to be laid on for the event to man the corner bar and to collect glasses.
- Additional staff would also be needed for the main bar, to cater for the extra people who might drink there before going to the disco.
- She would have to ensure that extra lager and shorts were available to cater for the extra demand. That was within her area of responsibility anyway and she would see to that personally.
- Thank heavens a late night licence was no longer needed.

Now, what else did she have to arrange:

- A carpenter for the stage
- An electrician for the sockets and the lights
- Additional staff
- Additional supplies
- Promotional arrangements
- The disco operators themselves

She needed estimates for the carpentry and electrical work that had to be done, together with a price from the disco operators, before she could work out whether it would be cost-effective to go ahead. She could supply the other costs herself.

Elaine had worked hard to prove to her boss that the idea should be adopted, and then even harder to ensure that everything was in place for the night.

The big night came and she was very nervous in case nobody came. She was delighted when all the old crowd turned up to drink in the bar together with many many more.

As the crowd continued to swell she had had her first misgivings. Her promotional mix had been a mistake, it had attracted too many people.

By the time the disco started there were already thirty people more than she had expected and they were still arriving. Most people did not arrive until after the advertised time.

Several things happened as she looked on powerless.

Some of the regulars, whose custom the event was aimed at preserving, were turned away because it was too full.

The only barman available for duty was Fred Holden, who was nearing sixty and was not exactly first choice for this particular task.

One barman was clearly not enough, and even though Elaine stepped in to help, it was a losing battle and the customers, forced to wait in a long queue, began to turn nasty. Fred, who was already at the end of his tether because of the loud music, lost his temper altogether. He swore at one of the youngsters and stormed off saying he was going on the sick.

Other revellers went off into the main bar and clogged that up so that regulars could not get a drink and tempers began to fray in there too.

The room was clearly too small for the numbers attending even though many had been turned away. This led to people dancing very close to the tables where people were drinking, and it was just a matter of time before someone knocked a table full of drinks over and the inevitable fight started.

At the sound of the fighting, the regulars in the bar gave up trying to get to the bar and decided to leave and go somewhere else for the rest of the evening. Luckily, it was late and there were not many of them left anyway.

Finally, in the scrimmaging, one of the disco operator's expensive record decks was damaged, causing them to pack up for the night and leave early, threatening to sue as they went.

'What a disaster!' Elaine repeated. 'Where did I go wrong?'

Let's look first at what was going on. This was a project because Elaine had to liaise with a number of different subcontractors and confront a variety of problems. She had a deadline to meet, within which she had to: carry out market research; and design the marketing plan using the Four Ps.

She then had to ascertain:

- What needed to be done
- By whom
- How much it would cost
- Whether it would be cost-effective
- Whether her boss would accept it

Finally, she needed to: put the arrangements in hand ready for the event; and run the event on the day.

So what did go wrong?

She had consulted everyone concerned along the way to ensure that they had the capability to provide what was necessary. What had she left out?

Well, let's look at the things that were not 'all right on the night'.

- The room proved too small for the numbers attending and there was no fallback position, such as an annexe which might have been opened.
- The numbers themselves had been badly misjudged, possibly due to Elaine's lack of experience in this sphere.
- The regulars had been inconvenienced and upset because the extra bar facilities were inadequate.
- Fred was really not the ideal person to have behind the bar

that night because: it was not really his scene; he was not adequately trained to deal with the sort of situation in which he found himself and simply could not cope.

- There had been no provision for dealing with any trouble that might occur.

The whole problem could best be summed up as one of lack of the necessary skill and experience to do the job. If we go back to the Otherwise analysis we notice that staff training was seen even then as a weakness and could have been *predicted*. Clearly, there is a weakness here that is preventing the organization from taking advantage of an opportunity.

As a supervisor it is vital to remember that your most important resources may well be your *Human* resources.

Element 2.1 is particularly relevant here, in that Elaine considered significant trends and made recommendations for the disco. However, it can be said that the most effective use was not made of resources, especially the human resources.

The fact that the latter was not done does not prevent it being useful as a learning experience. It may be used to compare subsequent performances to show what has been learned from the experience and will certainly be invaluable when looking at personal competences, some of which we will be looking at in the final chapter. We will see what Elaine learned in Chapter 5.

We can see that there is not the vital match here between what has been promised to the customer and the capability of the operations to provide it. As we saw in the previous chapter, this is likely to lead to customer dissatisfaction on a large scale.

Case Note 7

'I really thought it would be good here tonight, I'm really disappointed. I shan't come to this hotel again, not even for a drink,' were the words of one of the customers as she left the disco. Elaine recognized her as Julie, a woman of about 21, who had been coming here for months.

We will examine in chapter 6 what Elaine might do to encourage Julie and her friends to come back.

Now that we've looked at the various types of systems, let's now look at how the increasing use of new technology has affected the way such processes are carried out, to the benefit of both customers and organizations.

NEW TECHNOLOGY

The development of new technology has had a great impact upon the operations function. Computers are now used routinely in many organizations. Some of the ways in which they are used include:

Computer aided design (CAD)

The design process can be improved by using CAD. The effect of using different specifications or materials can be displayed graphically on the screen so that decisions can be made as to how best to satisfy the various requirements including those of the customer, the cost and any safety provisions. Lists and specifications of materials and parts may also be held on the system so that the best possible utilization can be gained.

Computer aided manufacture (CAM)

Computers aid the planning and implementation of the operations systems. They may be used, for example, to programme the switching of machines from one batch process to another. This allows a much more flexible and faster response to be given. They may also control robots which replace human involvement in repetitive processes such as drilling and welding, especially on production lines. Quality can be increased because of the precision with which such systems work.

Robots

Robots have been introduced in some manufacturing systems and have been found to be extremely effective. However, they do require a large amount of investment.

Real time computer systems

Real time computer systems are those which give an accurate picture of what is actually going on at the moment. Information is fed into them at regular intervals throughout the day (and night) so that they are continually kept up to date. This contrasts with other computer systems which tell you what has happened over the previous months or years, for example. In a real time system you can see what is actually happening as it happens.

There are a number of different real time systems used in a variety of ways.

In railways they are used to control the movement of locomotives and rolling stock. Each time they are moved the computer is updated to show their new position. Ordering them to a particular location is also carried out through the system. In addition, as soon as a wagon is emptied or loaded the fact is updated in the computer. British Rail have a very comprehensive system known as the Total Operations Processing System (TOPS).

In supermarkets they are used to control the amount of stock available in the store and on shelves. Here they are known as Electronic Point of Sale (EPOS) systems. Whenever an item is sold the fact is fed into the computer (usually by bar code reader) and the new stock position is updated. Again, the system is used to order supplies and can be used to monitor the rate of pilferage.

Computers are also used in other real time situations such as:

- railway signalling systems – allowing one signal box to cover many miles of track. The programming is set up to prevent conflicting movements being made during normal operation.
- computer reservations systems – which have given travel agents and transport organizations the capability to reserve seats, flights, hotel rooms etc. at the touch of a few buttons in the fraction of the time it used to take by telephone and letter.

The introduction of these real time systems, though they initially require considerable investment, may well lead to significant savings due to the increased amount of control they give the organization. They are also likely to lead to an increase in the quality of service that can be given.

A railway operator is able to inform a customer of exactly where his wagon of freight is at any given time. In addition, fewer wagons are likely to be needed to move the same amount of freight, because as soon as a wagon is emptied the fact is known and the wagon is immediately available for its next load.

Similarly, supermarkets are able to order stock far less time in advance, so it is likely to be fresher and the dates of manufacture of processed foods can be carefully controlled to ensure that items do not remain beyond their sell-by date. The costs of maintaining stocks in the warehouse are also considerably reduced.

The travel agent can now offer a range of holidays confident in the knowledge that he can quickly find out the up-to-date situation concerning availability, suggesting alternatives where necessary. Usually, the customer can walk into the agency and leave a short time later with flight or holiday selected and reservations made.

Management information systems

The ability to store and analyse huge amounts of data has given an enormous opportunity to many organizations.

Transport companies have information on where people are travelling to and from, the type of ticket they have bought, and the class. They can use this as part of their marketing research.

Local authorities have a record of everyone who should be paying Council Tax. The amount of money likely to be raised can be forecast in some detail.

The information can be used in many different ways, including analysing trends, planning or keeping records. We will be looking at the management of information in more detail in the next volume of *In Charge*.

SUMMARY

Supervisory Management Standards:

Unit 1   Maintain services and operations to meet quality standards
Element 2.1 Plan for the use of resources

There is a model that can be used to demonstrate the operations process.

Inputs are those resources and skills that go into the process.

Value is added to the inputs as they are transformed into outputs which lead to customer satisfaction or customer dissatisfaction.

Most outputs form inputs to another operating process.

There are five main types of operating system:

- Jobbing
- Batch
- Line
- Continuous
- Project

The type of system used will depend upon a number of factors.

New technology has enabled some organizations to gain better control over their operations processes, thus allowing them to reduce costs and increase the quality offered to the customer.

Chapter 3
Planning

We are now going to look at how resources can be managed effectively and efficiently. In order to do this we need to consider three stages: planning; organizing and implementation; and control.

In fact, these stages can be represented by the model shown in figure 3.1.

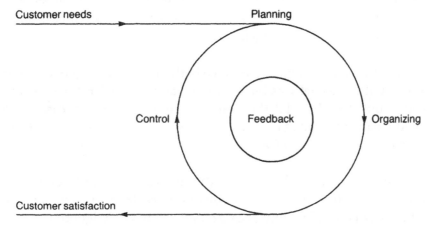

Figure 3.1 The planning, organizing and control cycle

Figure 3.1 shows the three stages in a continuous process revolving around the hub of feedback. We will be looking at feedback in chapters 5 and 6. It also shows the importance of reacting continuously to customers' needs in order to ensure customer satisfaction in an environment, which as we saw from our PEST and Otherwise analyses in chapter 1, is ever-changing.

In this chapter we will look at the planning stage, then we will go on to look at organizing and control in the next two chapters. Before we begin, however, let's call in at our hotel.

Case Note 8

Jane sat in the chair and pondered. She had been asked by Elaine to check that all the cutlery was clean for the wedding on Saturday. This was the first wedding that she had been involved in and she was a little nervous, especially after the fiasco of the new disco last week. Elaine had shown her where the cutlery was kept and she had set off immediately to carry out the task. Now that she had the cutlery in front of her it didn't seem such a straightforward job as she had first thought:

- She did not know how many people were coming;
- She had not been told what the menu was so she did not know which cutlery would be required: for example, fish knives or soup spoons;
- The cutlery was shining brightly and was clearly in good condition, but there were some marks on some of the pieces and she could not tell whether they were the usual marks of wear and tear caused by the dishwasher or whether they needed to be cleaned again.

There was no one around to ask since both Elaine and the head waiter were out and the chef was busy. There was nothing for it: she would have to put the whole lot through the dishwasher just in case. This would mean she would be late starting her next job which was setting the tables for morning coffee . . .

It may seem a very obvious fact that in order to **plan** to do something, we need to know what our **objectives** are. In fact it is so obvious that a lot of people in many organizations completely ignore it.

How often have you set off to carry out a task set by your manager, only to find that you are not really sure what you are meant to be doing? Oh yes, you thought you did, but now you're not at all confident that you know what is required.

And are you quite sure that your subordinates always know exactly what is required of them when you give them work to do?

THINK POINT

How can you ensure that staff always know what you expect of them?

You should state clearly what the task is, giving sufficient detail to ensure that the individuals concerned have enough knowledge to enable them to carry it out.

Remember, different individuals may need more or less information and guidance. Tasks that one individual may find stimulating and challenging may be found impossible by someone else.

The standard of performance you expect should be clearly stated, or even written down. Quality and performance standards will be discussed in more detail in a later chapter. The task must be achievable, and the person carrying it out should be able to measure when it is complete.

Limits of authority should be established so that your subordinates know when they can make their own decisions and when they need to refer back to you.

You should encourage people to seek clarification. A few moments making sure that everyone understands at the beginning will save a lot of wasted time and effort in the long run.

Whenever possible, agreement should be reached with the person whose objectives are being set. They should be encouraged to make suggestions and be involved in the objective setting process. This will help them to 'own' their objectives, which is the first vital step towards achieving them. It also allows them to give feedback during the planning stage, which may well bring about improvements to the original plan.

Objectives should be clear, measurable, achievable and agreed.

Element 5.1 of the Management Standards is particularly relevant here.

THINK POINT

How well do you think Elaine has performed in setting Jane the task of checking the cutlery?

She certainly needs to consider all of the points made above since she does not really seem to be doing any of them.

Most organizations state exactly what it is that they want to do. They usually begin with a **mission** statement which shows in broad outline what they are aiming for in a number of areas such as:

- Finance
- Customers
- Environment
- Employees

Thus, a supermarket might indicate that it wants to

- make a profit for its shareholders
- give high quality and value for money to its customers
- ensure that it does not sell or use anything which harms the environment in any way
- provide a safe and conducive working environment in which employees will have the opportunity for self-development to enhance their career prospects

All of these statements are broad indications of what the company wants to do. None of the statements are measurable, and it might be very difficult to judge from them whether the company has been successful in meeting any of these broad aims. Mission statements can usually be found in the Company Report, but good organizations will ensure that their employees are aware of them, usually by sending them a written copy or by publishing them on notice boards.

In order that the company might have something definite to aim at and to be able to judge whether they succeed, objectives are set in line with the mission statement. The important thing about objectives is that they should be measurable. So our supermarket might set objectives in each of the areas as follows:

- We seek to increase profits by 7 per cent over last year
- We will use a minimum of 95 per cent meat in all sausages
- We aim to ensure that all paper-based packaging materials are made from recycled paper by the end of 1993
- We will ensure that all supervisory staff will have attended a course on managing people within the next two years

All of these objectives are measurable and the company will know whether it has met them or not.

In order to meet the objectives choices have to be made. The decisions that the company makes in order to meet these objectives is called the **strategy**. Our supermarket may pursue the following strategies to fulfil their stated objectives:

- Buy a small chain of supermarkets who are offering competition
- Make all sausages internally rather than buying them in
- Cease all purchases of paper products that originate in rain forests and only purchase from managed forests or timber farms
- Agree that a pool of selected staff will be upgraded on a temporary basis to enable supervisors to be rostered to attend the managing people courses

These, then, are all ways in which the objectives might be achieved. Strategies are usually long-term and take the broad view of events. **Tactics**, on the other hand, involve shorter term reactions to factors that arise. Some tactics might be to:

- Reduce prices in the short term to combat a price war started by a competitor. Market share may thus be maintained
- Buy the sausages from a very quality-conscious supplier that they can trust, until the necessary equipment is installed to make their own
- Use alternative methods of packaging as far as possible until new contracts can be arranged
- Work overtime until the pool of staff is properly selected and trained

Usually tactics will be short-term and be a reaction to a situation, but they will still allow the long-term strategy to be carried out. To take another example from the football field: a manager may have the objective of winning the league next season. His strategy might be to attract this season a number of star players who will eventually be welded into a winning team, playing attractive football. However, he will still take note of each opponent on a game-by-game basis, and employ the tactics he feels are most likely to obtain a good result. To summarize then:

- *Mission*: a broad statement of intent made by the organization
- *Objectives*: should be measurable and achievable
- *Strategy*: long-term decisions to achieve objectives
- *Tactics*: shorter-term reactions

Once the objectives are agreed at the top level of management, it is possible to break them down into individual objectives for various departments. These departmental objectives can then be broken down until individual management objectives are set. All of the objectives should be complementary to the main objectives of the organization. If they appear to conflict then they should be re-examined and a strategy produced to resolve the situation. We will see later that one of the possible areas of conflict is between the operations and marketing functions.

Management by objectives has been extensively used in recent years but has gone out of fashion a little now. It is based upon managers agreeing with their subordinates a set of objectives that are measurable and achievable. Remuneration is often linked to the achievement of these objectives. This can be quite an effective system, but there are a number of dangers:

- the objectives may not be clearly defined
- they may be imposed from above and may not be achievable
- the manager may focus only on the set objectives and miss other important factors

P. F. Drucker (in *The Practice of Management*) identified eight areas in which objectives should be set. These are known as **key results areas**. The eight areas are:

- Market share
- Innovation

- Productivity
- Physical and financial resources
- Profitability
- Management performance and development
- Worker performance
- Social responsibilities

Contributions towards the meeting of objectives within the key results areas are identified for individuals and teams. The accent is placed upon the outcomes achieved rather than on specifying to people how they might achieve them. As a supervisor you may find that your manager has agreed key results areas with his boss. He may well discuss with you your expected contribution.

Supervisors need to be aware of what the organization's mission and objectives are. This will help you when making difficult decisions when there is no one available to give you advice.

Once we are sure what our objectives are, we can begin the planning process. First we need to decide what period the plan will cover.

It may be long-term and cover perhaps one or two years. The period will be determined by the industry you are in. The airline industry, for example, plans up to twenty years ahead, while a high-tech computer firm may regard six months as long-term. This plan will relate to the amount of work expected in that period. It will be used to decide upon the amount of fixed resources required, including:

- factory space
- machinery and equipment
- staff numbers
- the type of operations process to be used
- the type of new technology, if any

A number of other operations strategies will affect the long-term planning process. These would include whether

- to make part of the product or buy it from a supplier – there are cost and quality implications here and we will look at suppliers in more detail later
- to make only once an order is received or make and put into stock – some developers build new houses and then sell them, while others find buyers before they start

- to increase or decrease capacity – decisions often need to be made a long time in advance
- to renew assets that are approaching the end of their life – this may involve reassessing whether you still want to be involved in this particular activity or whether you want to hire or buy

One of the most important decisions to be made is the amount of the product the organization is to be capable of providing, that is, the capacity.

CAPACITY

This is very much part of the long-term planning process. The marketing department is likely to specify the anticipated demand over a period of two or three years and the operations should be set up in the most efficient way to meet it.

There is always going to be tension between the marketing department, who want the customer to have everything immediately, preferably in a choice of styles and colours, and the operating function, who are looking for long runs of standard products with the economies of scale that result.

In addition, demand tends to fluctuate. The forecasts may need to be broken down to show the spread anticipated during the year. It is not really possible to keep increasing and decreasing the permanent staff that you have on the payroll, nor to keep changing the number of machines you use every month, nor to change the size of the factory in order to keep up with these fluctuations. Fortunately, there are a number of strategies that can be used. These are:

- Smoothing
- Differential pricing
- Queuing
- Subcontracting
- Part-time staff
- Turning excess product into something else

Smoothing

The capacity is set around the average so that in months when production is greater than the demand stocks are built up. These are then used up during the months of high demand. This method is not available for organizations whose products are perishable, such as airlines.

Differential pricing

Airline seats are extremely perishable in the sense that, once an aeroplane is in the air, any opportunity to gain revenue from seats that have not been sold is lost for ever. They have to be sold before it takes off. Seats which remain unsold a short time before the date of departure are often sold off cheaply through specialist travel agencies. Holiday tour operators do much the same thing. One of the problems here is that customers will anticipate that there will be a reduction if they wait and therefore do not buy at the normal price. In the retail industry, people will hold off buying until a sale, when they know that bargains will be available.

Another form of differential pricing is that used by the railway and the tourism industries. Here, prices are set according to the anticipated demand in a period. For example, travelling into London during the rush hour will cost you full price, while if you wait until it is over your fare will be much reduced. This ensures that a high price is obtained by the organization when demand is high, while customers are encouraged to use spare capacity at off-peak times which would otherwise earn very little.

Holiday tour companies offer very cheap holidays during periods of the year which are not particularly popular in order to gain some revenue from hotels and transport that would otherwise be little used.

Queuing

Many organizations use this method. Queues are quite normal in banks and building societies. Most people also expect to queue in a supermarket at the checkout. There are usually targets set at what the organization feels that the customer will find acceptable. Once the queue becomes longer than that level, another window or checkout is opened until the queues recede. In the longer term, banks have tended to elect for single queuing systems, which appear to reduce customer frustration, while supermarkets are continually seeking ways of speeding up the checkout process. New technology is constantly being introduced, such as debit card readers, cheque writing machines and bar code systems.

There are other ways of being in a queue. Telephone queuing is extremely common. Busy airlines, theatres and travel agents use this system for dealing with reservations. Again, targets are usually set. An example of a target might be that 95 per cent of calls should be answered within thirty seconds. Sophisticated computer systems are available to monitor telephone response times.

You may also be in a queue while sitting at home. You may have ordered a piece of furniture and have been told that delivery will be in three weeks; or you may be waiting to go into hospital; or waiting for an electrician to arrive to repair your washing machine.

In most cases organizations are constantly looking for reductions in the length of time people have to wait. Appointment systems are becoming much more common, from the hairdressing industry to doctors' waiting rooms. Repair specialists are now offering the choice of morning or afternoon calls.

Subcontracting

It is quite common now for organizations to set their capacity at a certain level and to subcontract to another company any business that is offered over and above this. The main problem with this is that you have to take great care to ensure that the quality of the subcontracted product remains as good as anything produced by your own organization.

Part-time staff

More and more companies are relying on a core of trained part-time staff whom they call upon during periods of high demand. This is especially the case in seasonal industries. The tourism industry employs huge numbers of seasonal staff, as does the retail industry in the weeks leading up to Christmas.

Turning excess product into something else

Many industries involved in perishable products are unable to store the product for any length of time. They may well use differential pricing to some extent, but they may still be left with excess product. Strawberry fields, for example, have a huge glut of fruit for a very short period. Certainly, strawberries tend to become cheaper as the season advances. However, a large amount is used in making jam and other confectionery items. In the same way, the fishing industry will can or freeze large quantities of fish.

Once the capacity you want has been decided there are a number of factors which affect whether you achieve it. These include:

- the amount of machinery
- new technology
- hours of work
- size of the workplace
- the amount of transport available
- the number of telephone lines
- warehousing and storage available

You can treble the capacity of a one-shift operation by introducing three shifts, provided that there are no other constraints which prevent it. However, you may not have enough lorries available to deliver the additional product. On the other hand, you might increase the staff in a telephone reservation office but not have enough telephones for them to use. Or you might introduce a new computer program which will allow your staff to produce twice as many invoices in the same amount of time as before; but can your mailing system handle them?

It is important, therefore, for all parts of the operation to have the same capacity, or bottlenecks will arise and prevent the intended capacity from being achieved.

Decisions concerning capacity are rarely easy. If you increase capacity and the demand does not materialize you may well go out of business. On the other hand if you fail to anticipate an increase in demand and your competitors are ready, then the result may well be the same. Some decisions must be made well in advance. Airlines are already planning well into the next century.

Medium-term plans usually involve a much more detailed exercise and may cover something like the next two months or so. They may well be based upon known or expected orders and will deal with staff rosters, material required, machine hours that need to be reserved. They will also involve managing the strategies used for dealing with the fluctuations in demand that we have considered above.

Short-term plans deal with what will happen over the next few days or hours.

For example, railway operators have a timetable which is intended to cover the whole year. However, alterations need to be made to cater for situations that will arise, such as essential track maintenance, summer excursion trains or peak summer traffic. These might be planned a month or two ahead. Short-term and emergency planning takes place almost by the minute to deal with a whole range of situations that arise such as train delays, locomotive failures, and derailments and accidents.

As a supervisor you may well be expected to give some input into long- and medium-term planning, but most of your planning activities are likely to involve the short term, covering a matter of hours or days ahead.

Short-term planning often involves updating or making alterations to plans that already exist. This can often be more difficult than preparing plans from scratch, because you need to ensure that everyone who is involved in the original plan is made aware of any changes. You also need to ensure that you do not solve your own problems by transferring them to somewhere else in the system.

It is vital, therefore, to be aware of all of the people who will be affected by any of the changes you might make, particularly if this includes customers. A written list relevant to a particular type of situation is especially useful. In a period of disruption to normal working, you might find yourself extremely busy in dealing with the problem itself and not have the time to inform the people who it might affect. A written list will allow you to delegate this task to one of your staff, who can work through it and contact the appropriate people. An example from our railway operators might involve a train delay. A written list of people affected might include

- Passengers waiting for the train
- Station supervisors further down the route who may have connections to consider
- Supervisors of locomotive drivers and other train staff, because they might have to arrange for these staff to be relieved if the delay is particularly long
- Staff who control the allocation of locomotives and rolling stock
- Signal staff who might have to decide whether to allow another train to precede the delayed train
- Train announcers at stations

When passing on the necessary information it is important that it is communicated clearly and in a form that can be easily understood by the recipient. A scribbled note left on someone's desk might not be easy to read and may lead to misunderstandings. On the other hand, a beautifully, painstakingly written letter left on the same desk may not convey the urgency of the situation. A garbled telephone message might leave out some important facts, while a fax message may convey the urgency but it does not allow you to test whether the person has understood your message – they might not even have received it!

Special care must be taken in respect of communications with customers: they must be made aware of any alterations that affect them. They might not be very happy at the changes you have made, so you need tact and diplomacy. You might not even be able to make changes without their direct cooperation and agreement, and this is likely to be set out in any written contract that exists between them and your organization. We will be looking at communication with the customer in a later chapter.

THINK POINT

Identify a recent occasion when you had to make changes to plans at very short notice. Make a list of the people that you informed and state why they needed to know. Was there anyone who you did not tell who, on reflection, you feel ought to have been given the information?

Elements 1.1 and 2.2 of the Standards are particularly relevant here.

It is very difficult to say where short-term planning ends and implementation begins, because whatever you do has implications for what you do next, so in a sense we are continuously engaged in planning as we carry out our jobs. We will look in more detail at organizing and implementing work in the next chapter.

There are three stages in the planning process: **loading**, **sequencing** and **scheduling**.

Loading

Loading is the process of working out the resources you need to allocate to a particular job or task. It will usually be expressed in terms of

- material
- man hours
- machine hours

Sequencing

Sequencing is concerned with the order in which particular tasks are carried out.

Scheduling

Scheduling actually gives a time when the work should begin.

Case Note 9

Marc looked at the list for the private function. He quickly assessed the amount of time he would need to prepare each of the different meals. All of the starters were simply a case of assembling the ingredients and could be done shortly before they were required. They would spoil if prepared too early.

- Prawn cocktail
- Melon Surprise
- Bayonne Ham

The main courses would need longer. The lamb would take at least two hours to roast as they were very large joints. The fish would probably only take half an hour. The lasagne about an hour. The vegetables would take less than an hour, but he was aware that he would be quite busy an hour before the meal and so he would prepare them earlier, which would take him about forty minutes. The salad was best left until the last minute. The stock for the meat gravy would take about three hours and should go on early.

- Roast Leg of Lamb
- Baked Trout
- Vegetable Lasagne
- potatoes
- carrots
- peas
- cauliflower
- mixed salad for lasagne

The sweets would not be needed until later in the evening. The lemon pudding and fruit salad could not be prepared in advance, but the syllabub was all the better for it and he would get on with that early so it could spend some time in the fridge.

- Lemon Pudding
- Syllabub
- Fruit Salad

The cheeses were already on a plate in the larder and just needed to be taken out with the biscuits at the appropriate time.

- Leicester
- Stilton
- Brie

Coffee would be made up fresh when required.

He worked out how long the meals would take to prepare (loading) in his mind, and turned to a more detailed consideration of the order (sequencing) and the actual time the process had to be started (scheduling).

- make syllabub 3:00 p.m.
- make stock for gravy 3:15
- prepare vegetables 3:30
- put lamb in to roast 5:30
- cook lasagne 5:40
- cook vegetables 6:45
- cook fish 7:00
- assemble starters and serve 7:15
- prepare and cook lemon pudding 7:30
- prepare and assemble salad and fruit salad 7:45
- serve main courses 8:00
- serve sweets 9:00
- prepare coffee 9:15
- serve cheeses 9:30
- serve coffee 10:00

THINK POINT

Consider a task you have carried out recently. Can you identify the steps of loading, sequencing and scheduling?

The example above is a relatively simple one. However, batch and project systems can become very complex and these steps can be extremely useful. In continuous and line systems the steps are built into the system itself. In a car assembly line, for example, the car will spend the appropriate amount of time on one process before being moved along to the next process in the sequence.

So let's have a look at some techniques that might help us in the planning process. We can begin by considering the use of Gantt charts, named after their originator, Henry Gantt.

GANTT CHARTS

Essentially, the Gantt chart is a bar chart which gives a visual picture of the proposed plan. They can be used in several different ways, and we will look at two of them.

The first is in planning the use of resources so that the most efficient allocation is obtained. Figure 3.2 illustrates the allocation of

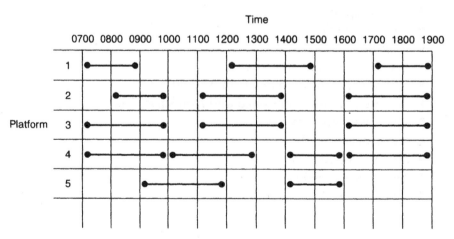

Figure 3.2 Allocation of trains to platforms over a twelve-hour period (Gantt chart)

trains to platforms in a terminal station. It assumes that the trains will have to be accommodated on the various platforms for different amount of times according to the amount of work (such as cleaning, etc.) that may have to be carried out on them.

On the left-hand side the resources to be used are shown – in this case railway platforms, but it could relate to different machines, for example in a manufacturing company. Across the top is shown the time, here hours of the day, but again it could relate to days or weeks according to the situation. The lines represent the planned occupation of the platforms between the times shown. Here, we can see that platform one is occupied from approximately 0700–0900, 1200–1500 and 1700–1900. Platform five, on the other hand, is only going to be needed from about 0900–1200 and 1400–1600.

We can see very easily how much each platform is expected to be used and where the opportunities are for further utilization. From the chart several points can be noted immediately:

- the two trains on platform five could be accommodated on platforms one (0900–1200) and two (1400–1600) respectively, calling into question the need to retain platform five at all. There may well be some other use to which it could be put.
- the peak times of operation can be seen, which appear to occur in the morning, around mid-day and in the late afternoon.
- it might be possible to allocate staff between platforms using the chart as a starting point.

The chart is not, however, the whole picture. For example, the platforms may be of different lengths and the trains scheduled for platform five may be too long to fit on any of the other platforms. There may also be other operating restraints: trains might only be able to approach the platforms from certain directions, so some trains might have to use certain platforms. In addition, trains may not run to time and platform five may be needed to accommodate those that are running out of order.

However, the chart is a useful guide showing the planned schedule.

Another use for the chart is shown in figure 3.3. In this instance a company has decided that a number of new machines are due to come into operation over the next few weeks. On the left-hand side are shown the activities that will be carried out to ensure that the machines will be phased in smoothly, while across the top is shown the time, in this case week numbers.

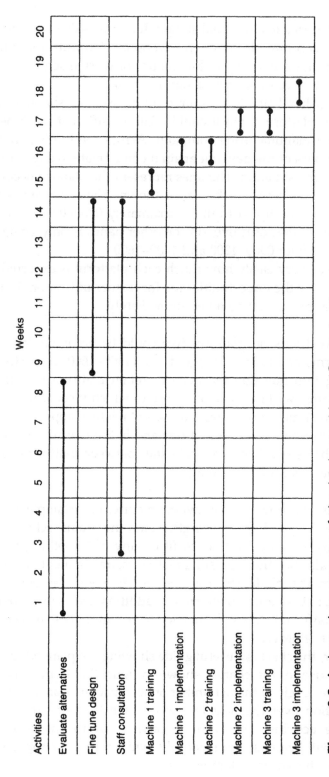

Figure 3.3 A planned programme of phasing in machines (Gantt chart)

The company begins by evaluating alternatives: this is expected to take eight weeks. Next the detailed design requirements will be discussed with the chosen supplier to ensure that they are compatible with the company's operations.

Meanwhile, the company will carry out consultation with the staff to obtain further information about any local design features that might be necessary, and to ensure that the staff are committed to the proposals. This will begin during the evaluation stage.

Once all of the design features are settled and the machines are available, they are scheduled into the programme. In this case the training will begin for the first team immediately after the decisions have been made. The first machine is installed the following week while the next team is being trained, and so on.

The steps of loading, sequencing and scheduling are quite clear here. The length of time each activity is expected to take (loading) is shown by the length of each bar. The order in which they are going to be carried out (sequencing) is manifest in the fact that the first machine will not be installed before the first team have been trained. Scheduling is the date at which the process begins.

This chart could also be used to show machines being installed against a deadline. Let's suppose that the end of week 18 was the date by which they had be installed. The chart would then be calculated back from that date to find out at what date the process should be started.

The progress can be monitored by marking on the chart another bar, parallel with the planned bar, showing the actual record of what is happening. If, for example, the evaluation process was complete by week four, a parallel bar would be drawn along the whole length of that activity from weeks one to eight to demonstrate that the particular process was finished and no further work is necessary on that activity.

Another planning technique is the combination of **network analysis** and **critical path analysis**, which are very useful in complex planning situations such as building roads or housing estates.

NETWORK ANALYSIS

Network analysis is an extremely powerful technique which can be used when planning complex projects or systems. It is based upon two factors:

- An **activity** is a period of action or waiting time that must occur before some other action can take place.
- An **event** is the action or occurrence following an activity and which depends upon that activity having been carried out.

Let's take a fairly simple example, such as buying and selling a house. Let's consider the events and activities involved:

It all begins with the decision to move house, which is the first event. There are now two main issues:

1 to find a house to buy
2 to sell the current house

These processes are linked to each other because people want to arrange them so that the sale and purchase take place simultaneously, permitting them to move from one house to the other on the same day. Let's consider the activities and events in each process and how long they might take.

Let's look first at activities and events involved in the purchase of the house.

- Go house hunting around estate agents
- See new house
- Consult building society
- Make an offer to purchase
- Apply for mortgage officially
- Building society survey must be carried out
- You may wish to arrange your own survey
- Own survey carried out
- Await results of surveys
- Mortgage is confirmed
- Find solicitor
- Instruct solicitor
- Solicitor deals with legal issues
- Exchange contracts
- Await final completion
- Arrange removals
- Inform gas and electricity etc.
- Arrange house insurance
- Final completion and move in

Although we have written down all the events and activities, we can in fact carry out some of them concurrently to save time. For example, we can arrange and instruct a solicitor as soon as we make an offer and he can be working on legal questions while we are arranging the mortgage.

Now let's look at the sale of the house:

- Look for an estate agent to arrange the sale
- Agree price required and put on sale
- Potential buyers come and look around
- An offer is received
- The offer is considered and negotiations take place
- The offer is accepted and solicitors are instructed
- Solicitors deal with the legal questions
- Contracts are exchanged
- Await final completion
- Arrange for gas and electric meters to be read
- Arrange removals
- Completion and move out

As we mentioned above, it is neither necessary nor desirable to wait until the purchase of the new house is complete before embarking on the sale of the current one (or vice versa), so both processes can be carried on at the same time.

We can now represent the project in diagrammatic form (see figure 3.4) using a straight line for an activity and a circle for an event.

It is also possible to show the length of time each of the activities is likely to take. This is our **loading** step.

We show each activity and event in the order that they need to take place. This is the **sequencing** step.

Scheduling might be involved in several ways. First it relates to the date when we first decided to move house. It also may apply to various points of the process. For example: completion should not take place on a Saturday or Sunday; removals would be difficult to arrange for on a Sunday; solicitors and building societies are not open on Sundays.

Our network diagram will look something like that in figure 3.4. The diagram allows us to see immediately what needs to be done before the next step can occur. It enables us to monitor the situation closely to see whether everything is going according to plan or is slipping behind. The way this is done is by monitoring the **critical path**.

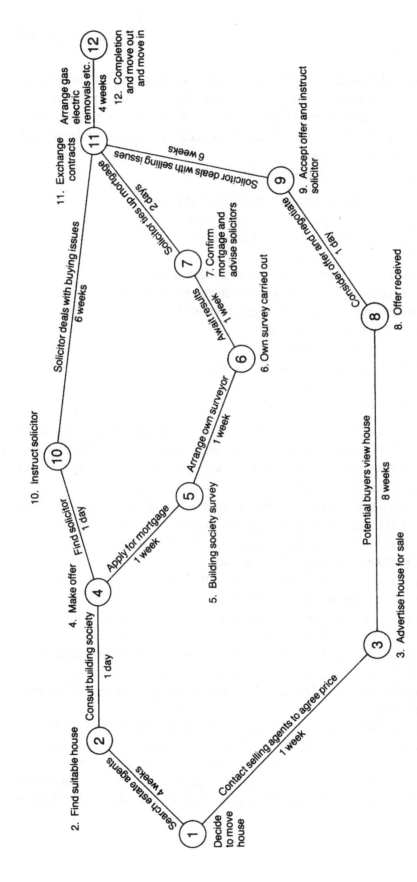

Figure 3.4 Moving house: a network analysis

CRITICAL PATH ANALYSIS

The critical path is found by adding up the amount of time taken to go along each route of the network. In our example there are three routes:

- 1–2–4–10–11–12 which takes 14 weeks and 2 days
- 1–2–4–5–7–11–12 which takes 11 weeks and 3 days
- 1–3–8–9–11–12 which takes 19 weeks and 1 day

The critical path is the *longest* route through the network, in this case 1–3–8–9–11–12.

The important point about the critical path is that this is the path which decides how long the project will take. Any time savings on any other path will *not* lead to a reduction in the overall time taken.

For example, if the legal issues concerning the purchase of the house take only four weeks rather than six, this will make no difference to the overall time of 19 weeks and a day. Nor would there be any difference if the surveys regarding the purchase were completed by the same person and available in one week instead of two.

On the other hand, if it took only five weeks to find a buyer then the overall time would be reduced by three weeks to 16 weeks and a day. If a buyer was found within one week, not only would the overall time be affected but there would also be a new critical path, which would be 1–2–4–10–11–12, and the time required would be 14 weeks and two days.

Just as there are no overall time savings unless they occur on the critical path, so time delays which occur on any other paths are not so significant.

Again looking at our diagram, a delay of three weeks in finding a house to purchase or in the time the solicitor took to progress the legal issues would not cause a delay to the completion date. A delay in finding a buyer, on the other hand, most certainly would.

We can also see that if we had gone on two weeks holiday immediately after event 4 so that the subsequent activities and events commenced two weeks later, this would have had no overall effect. This leeway is known as **float time** and is the time available to be used up before a delay is caused to the project.

Clearly, therefore, supervisory effort is going to be most effective when applied to the critical path, though of course too much delay on other paths will cause the critical path to change. You must also be aware of the float time available to you as this will help in the decision-making process.

Of course, major projects such as building the Channel Tunnel or a motorway are controlled by sophisticated computer programming, but they are based on these techniques.

SUMMARY

Supervisory Management Standards:

Unit 1   Maintain services and operations to meet quality standards
Element 1.1 Maintain services and operations
Unit 2   Contribute to the planning, monitoring and control of resources
Element 2.1 Plan for the use of resources
Unit 5   Contribute to the planning, organization and evaluation of work
Element 5.1 Contribute to planning work activities and methods to achieve objectives

---

It is important that staff know both what their objectives are and the standards that they are expected to achieve.

Objectives should be both measurable and achievable.

Planning the capacity of the organization is one of the most important aspects of operations.

Demand tends to fluctuate, so matching capacity to demand requires a number of strategies.

Gantt charts and network analysis are useful planning techniques.

Chapter 4
Organizing and Implementation

We've looked at planning and have already seen that there is considerable overlap between very short-term planning and actually doing the job.

Let's now consider actually getting on with the task that has been set.

'If all else fails, read the instructions!'

The first point to consider is whether you have been given any specific instructions to help you to carry the task out. These may come in several forms:

- Oral instructions from your superior or from someone who has successfully carried out the task before
- Written instructions from either of the above
- A procedures manual or instruction book
- A written contract between your own organization and a customer
- Verbal agreements
- An instruction video

Now, it is quite obvious that we should take necessary advice before we start, but it is equally obvious that not everyone does.

- When you last got into a car you had never driven before, did you read the instruction manual first? Some people find that the first time they open the manual is on the hard shoulder while waiting for the AA to arrive, or they find it is getting dark and they don't know how to turn on the lights.
- When you use a new video recorder for the first time do you bother to read the instructions first or do you assume that you know how to operate it?
- Yes, you're sure that Oldoak Ltd usually have the half-inch screws, so why bother to look at the records to confirm it.

Often, then, we just assume that we know how to do something and only when we run up against a snag do we start looking around for help. The information is often very easy to access and there really is no substitute for making sure.

Sometimes information is not readily to hand and it is no surprise, therefore, that people can find the barrier between themselves and the necessary information unbridgable. Some barriers include the following:

Records held on microfiche They often take time and effort to find. They should ideally only be microfiched when no longer needed for current operations.

Files not properly indexed This may result in a particular file not being easy to find. It is vital that all filing is kept up to date and in the correct order, both within the filing system and in the file itself.

Incomplete records Often a particular procedure or agreement may be so useful to a particular operation that the people concerned remove it from the master copy and keep it for their own use. Extra copies of the manual or photocopies of the relevant parts would prevent any problems.

Out-of-date records and instruction manuals Updating records and instructions is a very real problem, especially in an organization in which they change very rapidly. The most common instances are:

- No amendments are made at all and updates are simply lost or filed elsewhere
- Instruction manuals have several sheets of amendments stuffed among the pages, but none are entered at the appropriate place. Anyone who wishes to use the manual has to read through all of the amendments in case there is one which is relevant to the procedure they wish to use.
- Conflicting instructions are shown but not dated, so no one knows which is current procedure.

In all of these cases it is essential that someone is given the responsibility for entering amendments and updating procedures. This is not always easy, especially if a job is operated on a shift system so that no one person can be held responsible. This is often solved by making a particular shift responsible or by allocating the job to a particular person.

One other barrier that should be mentioned here is the **deluge of information** that is often sent out with no thought beforehand about who really needs it. Employees are sent everything whether it affects them or not, and they have to wade through page after page to try to find out if anything affects them in their particular job. The end result is that either

- they stop bothering to read them and therefore miss something important, or,
- they read everything thoroughly but simply miss something because of the sheer volume.

It is not always possible to get this just right, but many organizations simply send out material and then wash their hands of the matter with the thought that, well, we've sent it out, it's their fault if they don't read it.

THINK POINT

Does this ever happen in your organization? Can you think of any ideas that might improve the situation?

One of the ways of controlling information overload is to have a distribution list of the people who need various pieces of information. Another useful system is for a named individual to have the task of going through the information and highlighting anything that affects the department. Or information can be graded into necessary to know and nice to know and given different colours of which everyone is aware.

Whatever method you choose, it is not enough simply to send information out without giving some thought as to how easy it will be to digest.

A lot of the problems involved in misunderstanding information are the result of people not having sufficient time to read it properly. Let's now look at how we can use our time wisely to ensure that we get the most value from it.

MANAGING TIME

Time is a very scarce resource and it is vital that you use it wisely. It is important to remember that other people's time is crucial to them too, and we should be careful that we don't waste their time either. Let's look at some of the ways in which we waste time:

- Doing something incorrectly so that it has to be done again: errors cost time and money, and we will look at how to improve quality in a later chapter
- Taking a long time to reach a much higher standard than has been set and which is not required
- Talking for too long on the telephone wastes both your own time and that of the person to whom you are speaking. Some people become involved in long calls while they are also engaged in a small meeting with one or two of their staff, who simply have to look on in frustration while holiday stories are exchanged: this wastes everyone's time. Clearly, social niceties need to be observed, but they can be carried out fairly quickly if you put your mind to it!
- Failing to use time-saving equipment: there are so many devices available which are aimed at saving time, and many of them are becoming cheaper. There is little excuse for calculators not being available where they would be useful.

- Giving insufficient consideration to planning ahead so that some things have to be done twice: everyone has their own story of the local Council digging up the road one week, then the gas board, followed by the water company in the third week, though it probably doesn't happen nearly as much as we are led to believe; however, failing to plan ahead does lead to a vast amount of wasted time. You ask your assistant to go downstairs to the photocopier. Just as he has left, you find some more that needs to be done. As soon as he returns, you ask him to go back again. A little forward planning might have prevented the extra journey.

- Attending meetings which are not necessary: most meetings are arranged for a very good reason. Some, however, could be avoided. If you find that your diary is being filled up with so many of them that you have insufficient time to carry out your work, then you may be attending too many. You need to ask yourself whether:

    it is really necessary for you to attend
    it would be sufficient to receive the minutes
    someone else could attend in your place

- Preparing too far in advance so that events overtake you: it will depend upon the organization that you are in, but it is important that you do not plan in a lot of detail so far ahead that a lot of it needs to be altered and most of the effort you put in is wasted.

A lot of the stress suffered at work is caused by failing to manage time properly. Most people are bombarded daily with a whole range of items that need attention:

- letters that need a reply or action
- telephone calls that need urgent action
- tasks set by their immediate superior
- deadlines to meet
- staff problems
- breakdowns
- meetings
- customer enquiries

Clearly, you cannot deal with everything that you have to do at once. You need to prioritize. In order to do this you need to know when you are expected to have taken the necessary action: that is, you need a deadline. This will allow you to set aside a period of time for each piece of work that you have to do. A diary is an absolute necessity as it allows you to show the deadline and see at a glance where you can fit the work in.

You also need a clear idea of how long the job is likely to take (loading) so that you can allocate the correct amount of time to it. So we can now look at how work is measured.

In the case of some tasks it is very difficult to predict how long they will take: how long will it take to deal with a particular staff problem, for example, or how long will it take to return to normal working after a breakdown. In both cases a mixture of experience and intuition will help.

On the other hand, some jobs can be measured fairly accurately. A foreman in a garage which services cars will have measured how long on average the appropriate service will take in respect of a particular make of car. He knows how many he can complete in a day and takes bookings accordingly. Many companies have sophisticated systems for recording the length of time taken to do particular tasks in order to charge the customer for the time spent. Analysis of these records will often give a good idea of how long it takes on average for a particular job to be done.

Other methods of measuring how long jobs take include 'time and method' study, in which the performance of tasks is analysed to find out how long they should take and whether they are being done in the most effective way.

We saw in the first volume of the *In Charge*, series, *Managing People*, that F. W. Taylor was the first person to look seriously at how work should be measured. One of the experiments he carried out concerned the loading of various materials at Bethlehem Steel Works in the USA. When he began his experiment the men used the same shovel no matter what they were loading, be it sand, iron ore, coke, limestone etc. The load carried on each shovel varied enormously according to what type of material was being handled. Taylor worked out that the optimum load for a man to lift on the shovel to ensure a good day's work was around 21 pounds. Taylor therefore designed a new range of shovels for each type of material so that they would normally carry that weight. So the men would be issued with the appropriate shovel for the type of material they were working with at any time. Output increased several fold.

In fact, many of the improvements in working procedures come from studying the way in which jobs are done rather than the length of time that people take to do them. In work study both the time and method is recorded and analysed so that recommendations can be made. Let's bring Taylor's example up to date a little.

A little earlier we mentioned a photocopier which was in an office downstairs, and noted how time might be saved by planning in advance. If we analysed the photocopying done in that particular department we might get the following results:

- Number of journeys by various people to and from photo-copier per day: 20
- Length of time taken there and back, including waiting time for the photocopier to be free (excluding photocopying time): 10 minutes

This would mean that 200 minutes is being spent per day in wholly unproductive time, albeit by a variety of people. The analysis would allow us to consider several ways of making improvements:

- The department may be able to justify its own photocopier in its own office.
- A tray might be introduced where photocopying could be placed. It could be taken down by one person once or twice per day.
- Further analysis of the amount of time the photocopier is in use may reveal that most of the ten minutes is spent in waiting time and that there is a need for a second photocopier in the same place.
- Or it may reveal that this department makes more use of it than any other and the photocopier should be relocated there.
- It is possible that a lot of the photocopying is unnecessary and should not be done at all.

The layout of the working area is extremely important too. In this case people have to keep going up and down stairs, which not only increases their downtime but also increases the risk of them having an accident during their working day. It is also likely to increase the amount of time they spend socializing, as they are almost bound to meet other people during the journey and have a chat.

THINK POINT

Suppose you are installing a new kitchen for Jill, the breakfast cook. What factors would you take into account in the layout?

Here are some suggestions:

- Jill would want a drying bench next to the sink.
- She might want the fridge a little distance away from the oven so that the heat produced by one is not vying with the cold made by the other.
- The dishwasher would be within reach of the storage spaces so that it could be emptied without moving backwards and forwards.
- An eye-level grill would prevent her from having to keep stooping to check on progress.
- A see-through oven door would prevent the opening and closing of the oven and the resultant heat loss.
- Benches with no visible joins would avoid waste food being trapped there, and would thus be easier to maintain and more hygienic.
- Lighting over the work benches would prevent her being in her own light in respect of any central lighting point.
- The waste bin should be positioned so that it is convenient and no one will fall over it.

There are many other factors which you could probably mention. In the workplace it is important to ensure that the layout is efficient. This applies not only to manufacturing industries, where it is important that the correct relationship between machines is obtained both for efficiency and safety, but also in all other work areas, including offices, hotels and forms of transport. We will be looking at the working environment in more detail later.

Whatever method is used for deciding how long a job will take, you will need to consider which task you will tackle first and this means setting priorities.

SETTING PRIORITIES

Whenever you are arranging the priorities in your diary you need to be aware that emergencies can crop up at any time, and you should build in some leeway to cater for them.

As well as having a diary you should also keep a list of what you have to do *today*. As you carry out each task you can cross it off the list. Any other jobs you are given during the day will be added to the list. Anything that is not achieved should remain on the list for tomorrow. At the beginning of the next day you will add to the list anything that needs to be done that day from your diary. And so you carry on updating your list so that you always know what else you have to do.

Once you have set out your priorities you should work your way steadily through them without going off at a tangent to do something else, unless you have planned to do so or an emergency arises. In this way you will actually achieve the tasks that you have to do and you can tick them off.

Some jobs clearly can't be done all at once and you may need to do bits of several tasks each day. In this case you should plan them in this way and work through your plan. Eventually you will be able to tick several jobs off at once. It is enormously satisfying when you complete several on one day.

If you keep wandering off your plan to do little bits here and there, you will find that you don't actually fully complete any of the tasks, that this adds greatly to the stress and may lead to you feeling that you have not got control.

> In that instance you will find that you are not running the job, it is running you!

You have already covered leadership and delegation in the volume *In Charge, Managing People*. Delegation of work to the appropriate staff will help you manage your own time and workload. It is vital, however, that you give the necessary instructions and that you ensure that these have been understood. You must also be quite sure that the people to whom you delegate work have both the time and capability to achieve it.

Let's examine whether Marc and his colleagues achieved this in the case study on page 47 before he set off for the market.

Marc has given James the necessary information and advice to allow him to deal with any situation that is likely to arise. Marc has also given relevant information to Elaine to enable her to organize the staffing arrangements, and to James to enable him to look after the incoming order. Elaine has given the head waiter a guest list and seating plan.

Clearly, there is a good, informal relationship here which allows a good understanding to be built up. This is also shown in James' parting recommendation to Marc, as he was setting off for the market in chapter 2, to the effect that Marc should look at the pineapples. This indicates that Marc encourages people to make suggestions.

Marc has made a contingency plan in case the meat and fish are not of the required quality.

Arrangements have been made for James to check each item to make sure that it is there and of the required quality. James has also been told what to do if the order falls behind time and how much he should spend if he needs to put the contingency plan into operation.

They certainly seem to be working together very well.

In any consideration of the management of time and the setting of priorities, it is important to be aware of how easy it is to put off doing those things that you find difficult or in which you are not particularly interested. Let's now look at some of the ways in which we do this.

WAYS OF PUTTING OFF WORK

Everyone has their own tactics. It really is surprising how many there are, and it is possible only to mention a few below. You may well be able to list some for yourself.

- Making a cup of coffee before you start is probably the most common and is certainly the easiest to justify to yourself. After all, you've got a lot of work to do and you need this to get you going. Try to achieve something before you have your coffee, by promising it to yourself as a reward.
- Arranging and then rearranging your schedule in your diary can make a convenient substitute for actually doing any work.
- Starting to answer a letter and then realizing that you need to do some further research before you are in a position to do so, usually ends up with the letter being put to one side to be dealt with when you have more time. This strategy has the added

advantage that it can be used in conjunction with the one we have just mentioned, because you rearrange your schedule to fit it in at another time. Usually, the task of carrying out the further research is not allocated any specific time so that when you reach this particular letter again in your rearranged schedule you are in no better position to deal with it, and the same thing may happen again. So you need to ensure that you cater for any further research that may be necessary.

- When setting your priorities you list all the smaller and easier jobs first because you can get a number of them off your list and then you can concentrate on the larger, more important ones, to which you will then be able to give your full attention. This is a very attractive theory and is very popular. Unfortunately, you never do reach the stage where the decks have been cleared of all the minor tasks because new ones arise all the time. You need to set priorities by the importance of the task and the deadlines set, not by how easy or difficult they are.

Throughout this section we have talked about ticking tasks off as you carry them out. It is particularly desirable to have a written list of the jobs you have to do. You can then physically tick them off as well as mentally.

WRITING THINGS DOWN

No matter how good your memory is, it is unlikely that you will remember everything that people tell you, so writing things down really is essential.

You should write things down immediately before you forget.

One of the most important things to remember when doing any kind of task is to give attention to detail. Only by making a note of the information you are given is this possible to achieve. This is especially true of information received by telephone or face to face where there is no other record if you forget. When giving people information you need to bear this in mind too. Often it may be better to send a fax which serves as a written reminder or follow up the telephone message with written confirmation. Managing information will be covered in a later volume in this series, entitled *Managing Finance and Information.*

Writing things down is likely to prevent misunderstandings, but it is also useful when things do go wrong, since it is possible to trace back to find out where the problem arose in order to ensure that it does not happen again.

So far we have looked at planning what we are going to do and then actually doing it. Now we need to consider whether what we are doing is correct or whether we need to make some alterations. We need to know whether we have a problem or not. If we do, we need to identify what it is, what caused it and how it can be solved. This process is known as 'control', and will be the subject of the next chapter.

SUMMARY

Supervisory Management Standards:

Unit 1   Maintain services and operations to meet quality standards
Element 1.1 Maintain services and operations
Unit 5   Contribute to planning, organization and evaluation of work
Element 5.1 Contribute to planning work activities and methods to achieve objectives
Element 5.2 Organize work and assist in the evaluation of work

The most important factor is to know what needs to be done.

Managing time is vital if the supervisor and the team are to be effective.

Setting priorities is one of the most fundamental considerations in getting things done.

How people work is important in respect of both the time that they take to do a job and in the method they use.

Writing things down is the best way of ensuring that you do not forget vital details.

Chapter 5
Control

Supervisory Management Standards:

Unit 2   Contribute to the planning, monitoring and control
              of resources
Element 2.2   Monitor and control the use of resources

We need to make a distinction between things going according to plan (or not) and things being done correctly or effectively. The plan may be wrong and need to be changed. So everything can be going according to plan and an organization can still go out of business. Remember the PEST and Otherwise analysis we carried out in chapter 1. We must continually be amending our plans to take account of what is happening around us and any changing customer needs.

In the previous two chapters we have looked at planning and carrying out work. Control is the third vital factor in the continual cycle of planning–organising–control that we saw in figure 3.1 in chapter 3.

There are two parts to the control process:

- Monitoring what is happening and analysing the results
- Taking any corrective action that may be necessary

MONITORING

There are many ways of monitoring what is going on. Monitoring may be concerned with

- time taken
- resources used
- amount of product made
- income earned

- costs
- quality

Most organizations translate their financial planning into a budget which shows how money is expected to be spent over the year ahead. The actual results are recorded and compared with the forecast and decisions are taken about how to deal with any deviations from the plan.

Any organization which is involved in construction work will have a plan of how many units they expect to complete within a given time. Progress towards this will be compared with the plan to ensure that the targets are met.

Most sales representatives have targets that they must meet, and their actual sales are recorded and compared with what they were expected to achieve.

A supervisor might check on whether a task he or she has given to a subordinate has been completed yet; an engineer will check that the bolts being produced are the correct size.

The monitoring system used will depend upon several factors:

- The importance of the task
- The time available
- The technology
- Who is doing the monitoring
- Who is doing the task

In our examples above, the budget is likely to be monitored by the use of computer spreadsheets because it is of vital importance to the organization. This method will allow different scenarios to be fed into the system to show what would happen if a variety of courses were taken. A decision can then be made about what action to take.

A graphic display of the construction units actually completed, compared with what was expected, would allow people to see at a glance whether they were on target or not.

Sales figures are likely to be calculated by spreadsheet like expenditure budgets. However, we are all familiar with the use of wall charts and graphs to show the current situation.

The supervisor might walk over to the subordinate and physically see what the position is. How often this might be necessary would depend upon the level of skill and experience of the person carrying out the task. Actually talking to people and listening to what they have to say is a very good way of finding out what is going on. Feedback should be encouraged from subordinates, who should also be encouraged to make suggestions for improvements.

Feedback should not only be sought from staff within the organization but also from others who are connected with it, such as suppliers and, especially, customers. We will look at feedback from customers in the next chapter. A very useful way of obtaining feedback from within the organization is to have some kind of staff suggestions scheme which encourages people to seek improvements. People receive a lot of satisfaction and pride from seeing their ideas being put into practice.

It is as important that those ideas which have been rejected are not overlooked. Time should be taken to explain to those who have offered them why it has been impracticable to put them into effect. Remember, feedback is a two-way process! They should be encouraged to continue to make suggestions. In fact, 'encourage' is a key word when considering feedback. If, as a supervisor, you can create an atmosphere in which people feel that their opinions are valued and recognized, you are likely to continue to improve the way you do things and the results you get. Any problems can, therefore, be discussed and possibly solved very quickly.

If there is less time available, the telephone may be used to obtain an up-to-date report. Alternatively, there could be a system in operation in which, when a task is completed, the fact is reported on a work sheet and sent immediately to the supervisor.

The engineer might use a whole range of methods for ensuring the quality of the bolt. We will look at some of them in the chapter on quality.

When issues of safety are concerned it is essential that procedures are set up so that they **fail safe**. This means that if things go wrong, the result will be safety, rather than danger.

This is especially important in the transport industry or any organization involved in dealing with hazardous goods or processes. Here are some examples:

- If a railway signal becomes defective it will turn to red and the driver will stop. If it goes out altogether, the driver will stop. Even if it is dark the situation is covered because the driver must know the position of every signal on the route, so he is aware if one is not visible.
- Nuclear power stations are constructed in such a way that they can cope with worst case scenarios.

- An electrical system has built in fuses so that if there is a problem it shuts down before any danger can occur. Your own house is likely to have such an arrangement.

Monitoring enables us to find out what is happening, but the important part of control is to analyse why things are going wrong and then to take action to put them right.

TAKING CORRECTIVE ACTION

Action must be timely, effective and appropriate.

Monitoring is very important, as we have mentioned above. It must also be capable of allowing us to take action at the right time. A budget system which does not tell us anything until the end of the year would clearly be useless, as it would be too late to take corrective action. In order to ensure that action is effective and appropriate we may need to choose from a number of courses of action.

Most supervisors are faced with problems every day. Some require only a moment's thought while others take a long time to think through. Let's look at some approaches that may help in **problem solving** and **decision making**.

Before we look at solutions, we should first consider how we know we have a problem. After all, some people have a lot of problems but are not even aware of them.

Most can be anticipated and countered by careful planning. You know that you have a problem when things either do not go according to plan or the plan does not achieve the desired result. This assumes that you are carrying out the monitoring process which we have just mentioned. A good supervisor will be aware of problems that are likely to arise and will be able to identify them quickly when they occur.

The first step is to identify the problem. This is not always as easy as you may think. The problem you think you have may only be a symptom of another, greater problem. Absenteeism, for example, may be caused by boring working conditions. A poor sickness record may be the outward sign that someone does not get on with their boss.

So before you start to solve the problem be sure you understand exactly what it is.

Once the problem has been identified there are some techniques which may help in finding a solution:

- Experience may help you. What did you do last time and what was the result? If it was successful, then the same solution may work again. There is a need to be careful here because two problems which seem to be the same can in fact turn out to be quite different, especially where personalities are concerned. What is successful in respect of one person may well not work with another.

- You could take advice from other people who have experience, including your boss and your subordinates. People who are actually doing the job often have very good ideas about how it might be done better. Most organizations operate some form of staff suggestions scheme. This should not be considered as purely a formal process: the views of your staff will be continually useful on an informal basis.

- Looking at the problem from another perspective can be very helpful. We all look at the world in different ways and it can be very useful to see a problem from another side. The customer's perspective should always be considered, and during the operations process it is very easy to lose sight of this. Listening to customers and others who have a different view of the problem will usually enable you to find a better solution.

- Brainstorming with other members of your team is often useful in this respect. This means getting together as a group to think up as many ideas as possible in respect of the problem at hand. It allows possibilities to be explored that you might never have considered on your own. The main point about brainstorming is that ideas are generated during the initial period and recorded no matter how unrealistic they might appear. No criticism of any suggestions is allowed. Once the ideas have begun to dry up the team considers the merits of each idea. Very often a solution emerges as a result of a modification of one or more of the ideas generated. In such sessions 'synergy' often occurs, which means that the results achieved by the group working together are better than might have been expected had the group members worked on the problems alone. (Problem-solving groups such as 'quality circles' are becoming increasingly common in organizations as part of the overall search for quality. We look at these in more detail later in the chapter.)

- The scope of the problem needs to considered. Does it have implications for other people or does it only impact upon the people in your team? This will affect how you deal with it and the level of advice you might seek. You need to consider whether in fact it is really your problem and whether you have the authority to deal with it. You may find that you can only make recommendations and the problem itself has to be solved at a higher level. It is important to realize this at the earliest stage possible as part of the process of identifying the problem.

- Contingency plans are made by most organizations. This means that there are recommended or laid-down procedures for coping with certain types of problems. Most hospitals have emergency plans for dealing with major accidents, as do transport organizations such as airlines and railways. Manufacturing companies too will have a recognized procedure for handling breakdowns when they occur. In your home you will have a number of household appliances which state what action should be taken in the event of a failure.

- Contingency plans for large organizations are often practised in the form of drills to ensure that they are likely to work in the event of the real thing. Often a number of organizations combine in this test, as in mock rail disasters, when all the emergency services are able to try out their procedures too.

The greatest danger in the problem-solving process is that it is very easy to become locked into a solution at a very early stage. All subsequent decisions and actions continue to take you down this one route. All advice is sought from the one perspective and only people who are linked to this particular solution will be involved.

The way to avoid this is to consider alternatives. A short time spent looking at them may save a lot of wasted time later on. One of the alternatives may be to do nothing, because the problem has no long-term implications for anyone except your immediate team and it may be best not to become involved at this stage. You might then keep the situation under review and decide to step in when you feel that it is not going to be resolved unless you do.

Generating alternatives needs a systematic approach to the problem. You need to seek information, take advice, look at the possible outcomes of each course of action. Many organizations have computer models which they use to help them in this process. They feed in a number of scenarios and analyse the likely results of the various strategies they might employ. However, you do not need high technology to use this approach. You simply need to consider other possibilities beyond the obvious solution that first comes to mind.

Once you have considered the likely outcomes of these alternatives you are in a position to take a decision on which course to follow. However, few decisions are made in isolation. Your ideal solution may not necessarily be the most practicable for other departments or it may involve a lengthy implementation process which your organization simply cannot accept at this time. We all have to work within certain constraints, and some decisions may have an unacceptable impact on other parts of the organization. For example, your ideal solution may involve the purchase of a new machine. If the company can't afford it, a compromise solution may have to be found in the short term.

Such restraints, however, should not prevent you from looking for the best possible solution in the first place and looking for ways of making it work.

Case Note 10

The day after the disastrous disco Elaine was already making plans to retrieve the situation. She knew where she had gone wrong and had seen the results from personal observation.

This time there would be no mistake. She had a list of all the things that she felt had gone wrong and was determined to put them right.

She had not arranged for enough staff to be on duty and the one who was allocated the job was not the right person. She would now have three staff on duty from the beginning of the evening. Not only that, they were all young, enjoyed discos themselves and they would be really suitable.

She had set aside the main bar for residents and regulars only so they would not be bothered, and she would use the other bar as an overflow for those who were not dancing. This bar, too, would have an additional member of staff, and would be policed by a bouncer that she had hired for the night (not that she thought there would be any trouble, but just in case . . .).

She had also made her peace with the disco operator by promising to compensate him for the damage caused last time.

Now she was satisfied that the capacity problems were sorted out and that the next disco would work well. All she needed was some customers, and that might prove a more difficult problem

So Elaine has in fact identified the problems and taken action which she feels will solve them. We will see in a later chapter whether anyone turns up. . . .

Now that we have looked at the general principles of control, let's consider in more detail the management of quality, which is a vital element in the control process.

MANAGING QUALITY

Let's first consider what we mean by quality:

- A product should be what the customer expects it to be
- It should do what the customer expects it to do
- It should last as long as the customer expects it to last
- It should represent value for money in the customer's eyes

Each of these statements has one thing in common: it contains a reference to the customer. This is extremely important. However good an organization considers its products to be, it is the customer who will be the final judge and jury. This is because attitudes towards quality are very subjective.

When Coca Cola brought out the new recipe coke a few years ago, they considered the product to be of high quality. However, people found that it was not the taste that they expected and therefore did not buy it.

Value for money

An organization must use the marketing process to ascertain what the customer does expect and then try to provide it. One of the expectations will concern the price. Quality and price have a very special relationship. However much they might like the product and however much they have available to spend, the customer is unlikely to buy if they consider that the price is too high.

Case Note 11

Marc had recently revitalized the menu in the restaurant in an effort to compete with the new restaurant which had opened nearby. He had introduced several exciting dishes, which had seemed to go down very well. The pheasant, the guinea fowl and the partridge pie were all very popular and he was very pleased with them, especially as it made the job more interesting for him and his assistant.

However, there was one dish that really had not got off the ground at all and had never once even been ordered: this was chicken made with his own special sauce, the main ingredient of which was a fairly expensive white burgundy wine. The dish was more expensive than the other chicken dishes on the menu and almost as much as the other new additions already mentioned.

He made up a questionnaire about the menu to find out people's reaction to it. He asked them a number of questions concerning the meal that they had chosen and invited them to make comments about the other items that they had not selected. Several customers expressed the view that the new chicken dish seemed a little on the expensive side when compared to other dishes on the menu. After all, it was only chicken!

He decided to use a much cheaper wine and reduce the price so that it was in line with other chicken dishes. It soon became one of the most popular meals that he served.

THINK POINT

Consider a purchase you made recently. Which was more important: cost, quality or value for money?

Design and conformance quality

It is often considered that the more you pay the better quality you receive. It must be remembered that the price depends upon what people are prepared to pay for the product. Often they are prepared to pay a little more for extra quality features.

Often the supplementary features of a product will make it

attractive to the customer. Most of the major airlines will transport people safely and reasonably punctually to their destination. People are likely to make their choice of airline according to the extras that each one offers, such as quick check-in procedures, complimentary limousines or a separate first-class lounge. It is interesting to note that most of the publicity surrounding the privatization of British Rail centres round the additional quality features that are likely to be offered, such as videos and in-seat catering, rather than any improvements in reliability or punctuality that might be achieved.

It is also thought that a good quality product costs more to make than one of slightly inferior quality. This is often true, because the ingredients may be more expensive or cost more to produce. However, it does not have to follow. Some organizations are able to produce very high quality at relatively low cost by ensuring that their operating systems are extremely efficient. Japanese manufacturers are a case in point. Their systems are extremely efficient and their focus on quality reduces waste to infinitesimal proportions, thus reducing costs even further. Many organizations in the UK and Europe are now focusing on and achieving this high quality at low cost.

In some situations, quality may be perceived by the customer as relatively unimportant. People on a limited budget may prefer to buy a used car rather than a new one, even though the quality may not be as good. However, as long as it satisfies what they expect from it, they will consider it to be good value. It should look in good condition, work without breaking down and last a reasonable length of time.

There is always a danger when talking about quality of assuming, because something is being sold on its budget price rather on any claims of quality, that quality does not matter to the customer or organization concerned. What we have been talking about so far has mainly concerned **design quality**, that is, quality features that the customer may or may not want.

However, a hatchback is not necessarily of inferior quality to an expensive sports car. It is simply aimed at a different market. It is just as important to the manufacturer of the hatchback that the product meets all of their own quality standards.

In the same way, budget-priced supermarkets are as keen to provide a quality service as those at the more expensive end of the range.

This is known as **conformance quality**; that is, how near the product approaches the specification laid down.

So, in our example above, Marc has reduced the price of the new chicken dish by using a cheaper wine and has thus lowered the design quality. But, although the dish tastes differently, it can conform to the new design and still be of very high quality, as its subsequent popularity proves.

As we mentioned above, it is important that any organization finds out what the customer expects and then sets out to produce it. Products will then be designed to meet these requirements. In order that an organization can be sure to constantly meet the customers' expectations it is necessary to set standards that must be achieved consistently.

Quality standards

Standards can be applied in many ways. They may relate to:

- Quantity – as in the number of matches in a box
- Time without failure – as in the running of an aeroplane engine in service
- Time within which – as in the length of time within which a letter will be answered
- Size – as in the length of a screw or nail
- Appearance – as in whether a new car has any scratches or visible damage
- Strength – as in the amount of pressure that can be applied to a girder before it breaks
- Keeping to contracts – as in providing holidays that are exactly as promised in the brochure
- On time – as in delivering a product when you promised
- Taste – as in food in a restaurant being enjoyable
- Trust – as in whether customers are happy to deposit their money in a particular bank or building society.

All of the above are measurable – even the last two, in the sense that food may taste anything from poor to excellent, and most people if asked would be prepared to give a rating, while trust either exists or not as the case may be.

Most organizations will have a policy concerning quality. *It is important that this is conveyed to the employees.*

THINK POINT

Do you know what your organization's policy is in respect of standards and quality issues?

British standards

The British Standards Institute has for many years been setting standards which products are expected to reach. In addition, there are European (EN) and International (ISO) standards which are in many cases broadly equivalent to the British Standard (BS).

Some examples of the standards that various products should meet are listed below:

BS 5423 is the specification for portable fire extinguishers (it is related, but not equivalent, to EN 3)

BS 5940 is the specification for the design and dimensions of office workstations, desks, tables and chairs

BS 2481 relates to typewriters:

- Part 1 is the specification for keyboard arrangements (it is related to but not equivalent to ISO 2126, ISO 2530 and ISO 3243)
- Part 2 is the specification for function key symbols (it is equivalent to ISO 1090)
- Part 3 is the specification for the layout of printing and function keys (it is equivalent to ISO 1091)
- Part 4 relates to the glossary of terms (it is equivalent to ISO 5138/9)

BS 5665 relates to the manufacture of toys (it is equivalent to EN 71)

BS 5750

BS 5750 was introduced in 1987 to provide a standard for quality management systems that could be attained by any company whatever its size or product. It has become the model for the equivalent

European Standard EN 29000 and International Standard ISO 9000. Because of this, any organization that is registered to BS 5750 can also claim approval under these standards.

It identifies basic systems that a quality organization should have and uses various criteria which are independently assessed. The following procedures and points are laid down:

- the organization's policy towards quality for its customers
- who is responsible for what
- how to ensure that the standards are met and the action to be taken if they are not
- the management representative responsible for ensuring that the system is implemented
- a continuous audit process to ensure that the system improves
- a procedure for establishing that all supplies and subcontractors meet the appropriate standards.

There are three parts to the BS 5750 process:

- Part 1 is used when the organization is able to design products. This activity is included in the assessment. A company which both designs and produces cars would be an example.
- Part 2 is used when the product is made to the customer's or to a published specification. A company which prints out pages that have already been designed by its customer would be an example here.
- Part 3 is not used very often, as it applies to organizations which are very simple and whose quality can be established very easily by a simple final check. A self-employed gardener would be a case in point.

BS 5750 is becoming increasingly important as a marketing advantage, since many organizations will only use suppliers or subcontractors who comply with its procedures. Without it, therefore, markets are becoming more and more restricted, and this trend is likely to continue.

In addition, the process of conforming to the Standard is likely to result in systems being put into place which will bring about improvements in the quality of the product supplied and reductions in the costs involved.

Standards and objectives

We talked in an earlier chapter about setting objectives for your subordinates. They need to know what they have to do, but they also need to be aware of the standard that you expect them to reach. These standards should always be measurable. Phrases to be avoided are:

- As soon as possible
- About three feet
- As many as you can by the end of the day

None of these allow the person to understand exactly what is expected of them. You should use instead:

- By three o'clock
- Three feet and one inch
- 30 by the end of the day

This also gives your subordinate an opportunity to inform you if he or she does not feel that the standard is achievable, and allows discussion on how it might be achieved in some other way.

As well as ensuring that standards are set it is important to ensure that everyone is aware of their individual responsibility in meeting them. We know from motivational theories (discussed in chapter 5 of *In Charge, Managing People*) that the more responsibility people have, the more likely it is that they will respond to the challenge of meeting the standards laid down. However, it is not enough simply to give them additional responsibility, they will also need to be given additional training to help them to meet that responsibility.

In addition, whenever responsibility is passed on the appropriate authority should go along with it. People cannot be expected to achieve a standard if they are not able to exercise the authority that is necessary to achieve it. The limits to this authority should be clearly specified so that the person knows when she or he needs to refer the matter upwards.

The further down the organization that responsibility can be passed, the more flexible the organization is likely to be in its response to the needs of customers, who do not want to wait until their problems are referred up to the managing director and back down again.

THE EXCELLENT ORGANIZATION

Peters and Waterman, in their book *In Search of Excellence*, identified eight attributes that an excellent company was likely to possess. These were:

1 'A bias for action' – know what the objectives are and get on with achieving them.
2 'Closeness to the customer' – the customers' needs should pervade all the systems throughout the organization.
3 'Autonomy and Entrepreneurship' – push responsibility down the organization and encourage people to respond to the customer. Mistakes are likely to be made, but these should be tolerated in the interests of flexibility and can be mitigated by additional training and clear limits of authority.
4 'Productivity through people' – excellent organizations will value their workforce and regard them as a good investment for the future. They are likely to ensure that excellent training is available to improve the all-round quality of their staff.
5 'Hands on; value driven' – all levels of management are seen to be in touch with one another. Managers are usually highly visible and are prepared to listen to problems raised at the shop floor.
6 'Stick to the knitting' – concentrate on what you are good at rather than expanding into areas where the organization has little experience.
7 'Simple form; lean staff' – complex administration systems and large hierarchies should be avoided. HQ staff should be relatively small, with most responsibilities being pushed downwards.
8 'Simultaneous loose–tight properties' – strong central direction on certain core values should complement the authority passed down to lower levels of the hierarchy.

As can be seen, several of these attributes involve the notion of ensuring that staff are encouraged to exercise responsibility at a level that is very close to the customer. The systems in place should support and encourage this by investing in training and improving communication, ensuring that everyone throughout the organization is aware of both the overall objectives and their own role within them.

Indeed, the role of people in the search for quality is crucial, and this vital task is dealt with in *In Charge, Managing People*. In this chapter, however, it will be useful to look at how people can be extremely effective in 'quality circles' or problem-solving groups.

QUALITY CIRCLES

Many organizations are now using quality circles in their approach to quality. They are usually composed of between five and twenty employees under the guidance of a supervisor or manager and meet regularly to discuss particular quality issues. A problem may have arisen concerning an engine that is incurring an unacceptably high failure rate. The group will analyse the problem and seek solutions.

It is important that the group is voluntary since it is unlikely to work effectively if coercion is used. Quality circles are also a good method of gaining employee participation, though they should not be introduced primarily for this purpose because they are unlikely to remain together if that is the main reason for their introduction.

Quality circles are usually introduced as part of an integrated approach to quality called 'Total Quality Management'. We can now have a look at this approach in more detail.

TOTAL QUALITY MANAGEMENT (TQM)

Total Quality Management is seen now by most organizations as the way ahead for the future. More and more are adopting this approach.

The key to TQM is that everyone has the responsibility for achieving quality, no matter what job they are doing or how close to or far away from the customer. Quality is sought in every area, from answering telephones to ensuring that the workplace is tidy. Each job, no matter how remote it may seem from the external customer, is viewed as being an essential part of the final product. If everyone in the organization lives up to their own individual quality standards then the end product will be total quality for the customer.

The approach has to be led from and supported by the top level of management, as it is all embracing and should pervade the whole organization. The main difference between TQM and other attitudes towards quality issues is that under TQM problems should be found before they occur (i.e. a 'proactive' system), rather than put right after they have happened (a reactive system).

Previous policies have been aimed at finding out where faults occur and then trying to solve them. TQM aims at a right-first-time approach. As well as involving quality circles, the TQM approach also incorporates the following:

- *The use of quality ingredients and components.* This may mean selecting suppliers very carefully or making your own. We will look at this aspect of materials management in a later chapter.
- *The emphasis on quality characteristics in the design of the product.* Organizations involved in TQM are likely to identify and stress those aspects of the product where quality is important. Thus Andrex place a great emphasis in their advertising on the strength of their products.
- *Training staff.* This is crucial for the reasons already mentioned above.
- *Employee relations.* Teamwork and employee responsibility is a central part of the policy. Each member of staff knows exactly what he or she is expected to do. In Japan, security of tenure is a regular feature of an employee's contract of employment. In other countries there is often an agreement that there will be no compulsory redundancies for a specified period. This allows employees to grow within the company without the fear that they will lose their jobs, and develops loyalty and trust between the management and employees. It may also free the staff from fear of repercussions should they try out something new that does not work, and therefore stimulate innovation within the company.
- *Continuous improvement.* Everyone is geared up continually to look for improvements in the way they do things. This is often very threatening to some employees who consider improvements as a kind of implied criticism that they were not doing their job properly beforehand.
- *A change in culture.* The whole way of thinking about how jobs should be carried out is altered. This often involves a major change in culture and must be supported by top-level management.
- *Attention to detail.* Giving attention to detail is likely to give you the competitive edge in many situations. Often it is the apparently insignificant things that can annoy the customer. Many organizations address the customer by name to show how much they value them. This can be a very effective way of

building up customer loyalty. However, call him/her by the wrong name and you are likely to offend the customer greatly.

- *Looking for solutions rather than trying to apportion blame.* In some organizations a lot of time is spent in trying to ensure that whatever happens it is someone else's fault. A lot of time is wasted trying to shift the blame somewhere else. The best way of avoiding mistakes is never to do anything, that way you can't do anything wrong. Some organizations suffer from this kind of paralysis because the employees feel that it is better not to attempt to do anything rather than be held responsible if things go wrong. If we look back at our excellent organizations, however, we find that one of the attributes is 'a bias for action'. An organization really interested in quality will support its employees when they make mistakes and use them as a learning experience. For every new product that is successful there may be a number that do not make it. An organization that has no failures may have no innovation.

As mentioned above, some organizations are able to produce high quality at a relatively low cost, so let's consider the relationship between cost and quality.

COST AND QUALITY

While striving for high quality may well lead to some increased costs, there are likely to be some considerable savings too. Costs of quality can be summarized as follows:

- More expensive materials
- Extra training for staff
- Increased inspection costs
- Devolving authority is likely to lead to people using it and thereby increasing some costs at the customer level (for example, an increase in the level of returned goods accepted)

Savings made by seeking quality:

- Getting things right first time, thus avoiding:

  waste materials
  wasted time in solving the problem
  wasted man and machine hours in doing it again

- Low level of rejection from the customer avoiding the need for:

  additional transport
  complaints procedures
  refunds
  compensation
  marketing effort to redeem the loss of reputation
  expensive repair and after-sales service

So pursuing a policy of striving for quality may well reduce costs overall rather than increase them.

Striving for quality is one thing, but how can we ensure that we actually achieve it?

CONTROLLING QUALITY

One way to ensure quality is to check every single item that is produced. However, this is neither desirable, due to the high cost of doing so, nor is it always possible, because in some cases you might have to destroy it to prove that it meets the standard for toughness (a steel girder for example), while in others the customer receives it as it is being produced so it is already too late (as in giving a haircut).

Where health and safety are involved a 100 per cent check is sometimes necessary, and such checks are likely to be built into the costs. In any case, competitors will be faced with making similar arrangements, so there is unlikely to be any price disadvantage. Fire extinguishers are a good example of this.

For most products, however, a statistical sampling system is used. It is much cheaper and more practicable. Sampling involves checking a random number from a particular lot or batch and either rejecting or accepting the whole lot on the basis of the results obtained.

Products have characteristics which can be considered in two groups: variables and attributes.

VARIABLES

Variables are those which can be measured in respect of height, weight, viscosity etc. These will be rejected if they do not fall within acceptable limits.

Attributes

Attributes are those which are not measured exactly and may require some degree of judgement. These include appearance, taste etc. They will be rejected if they have flaws that can be seen or the taste is not acceptable.

There are also two main types of sampling: process sampling and acceptance sampling.

Process sampling

Process sampling means that the product is sampled as it is being made so that any defects will be spotted and corrected. Marc, our chef, is likely to do this as he cooks his meals. No doubt he will taste the gravy and alter the seasoning as necessary before any is served.

Acceptance sampling

Acceptance sampling is carried out when the product is completed and available for the customer. Having made and cooked several steak and kidney pies, Marc might open one up and taste it to ensure that they are up to standard.

How much sampling should be carried out will depend upon a number of factors. The greater the size of any sample the more accurate will be the results. In some manufacturing processes where hundreds of items are produced each hour, a random number may be selected for testing each hour to ensure that the quality is within acceptable limits.

However, the more sampling that is carried out the greater the cost. Usually the degree of risk to the organization is taken into account. If the overall costs of faulty products, including repairing them or giving compensation, are likely to be high, then more rigorous inspection may be the best policy, as it is likely to prove cost-effective in the long run.

Where a large number of items are being sampled on acceptance, because of the costs associated with inspection, it is usual to agree between customer and supplier a figure which is the acceptable quality level (AQL). This might relate to the amount of defective items in a batch. For example, in a batch of one thousand items it may be decided that the sample size will be one hundred and that two defective items in that hundred would be an acceptable percentage. This means that any batch which is two per cent or less defective is likely to be accepted.

At the same time a tolerance figure is also agreed, the Lot Tolerance Percentage Defective (LTPD), which is the lowest level of quality that is likely to be accepted. If this were set at five per cent, for example, any batch where the sample showed a higher amount of defective items than that would be rejected.

In service industries and others where the customer is actually involved at the point of production, spot checks can be carried out. This might involve a manager ringing up her own organization to check whether the telephone response time is being met. Or another manager might take one of his airline's flights and check whether the service level is meeting the required standards.

Should problems arise either during the process or during acceptance sampling, then they need to be solved using any of the problem-solving techniques discussed earlier in this chapter. However, there are two more techniques which might be useful, and they are:

- *Pareto analysis*, named after the Italian economist Vilfredo Pareto, who first made his observations (summarized below) in 1906, which we will meet again and in more detail when we look at the management of materials; and:
- *A cause and effect diagram*, also known as an Ishikawa Diagram, again named after the person who first used them in Japan in 1976.

Pareto Analysis

Pareto observed that in any group a relatively few items made up the most significant part of the group. This significant few may mean that some 80 per cent of the faults or problems that occur may be caused by only a small number of types of defect. Focusing on these particular types of defect and finding solutions may prove particularly cost-effective, as they will remove most of the problems that you have.

Cause and effect diagram

When the types of defect have been identified, the cause and effect diagram will assist you to find solutions.

The problem is shown at the right-hand side of the diagram and then possible causes are written into the diagram in a kind of fishbone effect. Each of these causes are then broken down still further until a number of possible causes are identified. Each of these can be examined in turn until the source of the problem is found.

Let's have a look at a possible cause of problems that might be occurring at a travel agents. The example giving out wrong information (see figure 5.1).

Each of the possible causes of the problem can be investigated to find out why incorrect information is being given.

THINK POINT

Let's consider some of the things that our hotel might need to introduce if it were to adopt a TQM approach.

Change in culture – already there seems to be a fair amount of responsibility passed down to the staff (Elaine and Marc for example) who are close to the customer.

Staff training – there does seem to be a need for some more training to equip the staff to take on their responsibilities. Elaine, for example, really did not have the experience to set up the disco on her own, and some guidance from above would probably have been helpful. Also, her management of her subordinates is not yet fully developed and more training in managing people might be useful.

Attention to detail – this is likely to be achieved as a result of increased training.

Continuous improvement – certainly there does seem to be a policy of everyone learning from mistakes to ensure that they are not repeated. There does not seem to be a proactive attitude to getting things right the first time, however. A quality circle approach might improve the situation, especially as at the moment everyone seems to look after their own problems and try to solve them without necessarily bringing in the views of other people who might be involved.

Employee relations – there do not seem to be any particular problems between any of the employees or between the staff and the management. There are no signs, however, of the security of tenure of jobs.

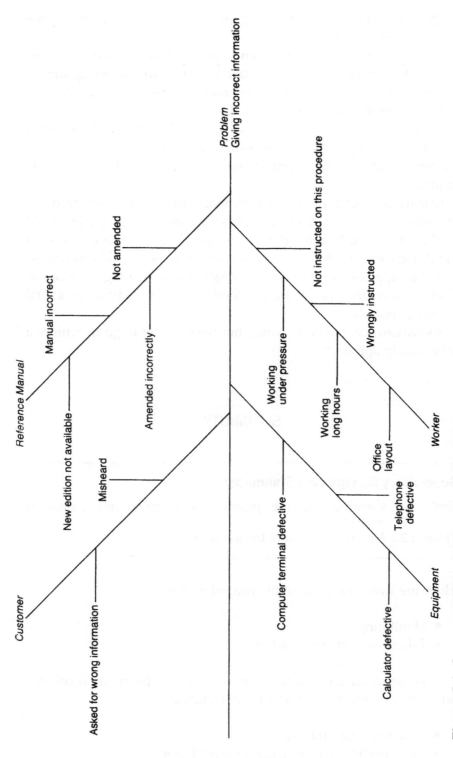

Figure 5.1 Cause and effect diagram: a travel agent

Quality components and ingredients – there is every sign that the policy is one of high quality.

Quality characteristics in design – clearly these are seen as desirable, but the customer decides. Marc increased the design quality of the menu in response to customer demand, but reduced it in one area when he saw that it was not wanted.

Looking for solutions – there does seem to be a atmosphere where solutions are sought rather than blame passed. Elaine has been able to continue with the disco project rather than being blamed for its failure.

Quality throughout every department – there does seem to be an attitude of quality in the departments we have seen. In the breakfast kitchen, the toaster suffered a malfunction but the sprinkler system did its job correctly. Again, in the kitchen, there seems to be as professional an approach to the clearing of tables and washing of dishes as there is to actually preparing the food, which is evidence of a total quality approach.

As we can see, the hotel would not have too far to go to achieve a total quality approach.

SUMMARY

Supervisory Management Standards:

Unit 2   Contribute to the planning, monitoring and control of resources

Element 2.2 Monitor and control the use of resources

There are two main parts to the control process:

- Monitoring
- Taking any corrective action

There are a variety of ways of monitoring and the method selected will depend upon a number of factors, such as:

- How important the task is
- How much time is available to carry it out

- When the results need to be available
- What technology the organization has

Action needs to be timely, effective and appropriate.

There are a number of techniques that may be used for solving problems and deciding on the right course of action.

Standards must be laid down so that everyone knows exactly what they have to achieve.

Managing quality is a vital part of the control process.

Design quality relates to the features that the product may offer.

Conformance quality relates to how close the delivery of the product comes to meeting the design specifications.

Excellent organizations are likely to have certain attributes in common.

Total Quality Management is becoming increasingly popular as a means of ensuring quality to the customer.

Chapter 6

Communicating with the Customer

Supervisory Management Standards:

Unit 1   Maintain services and operations to meet quality standards

Element 1.1 Maintain services and operations

1.2 Maintain the necessary conditions for an effective and safe environment

Unit 2   Contribute to the planning, monitoring and control of resources

Element 2.1 Plan for the use of resources

2.2 Monitor and control the use of resources

Unit 5   Contribute to the planning, organization and evaluation of work

Element 5.1 Contribute to planning work activities and methods to achieve objectives

5.2 Organize work and assist in the evaluation of work

This chapter has relevance to most aspects of units 1, 2 and 5. There are some performance criteria which relate specifically to the customer. However, references to the customer appear throughout the Management Standards and it is the purpose of this chapter to give an understanding of the interaction that takes place between an organization and its customers which will be useful throughout all of these units.

The first contact that the customer has with most organizations is usually as a result of the marketing initiative. This may be because they have been attracted by

- television or newspaper advertising
- a display or special promotion in the store

- telephone
- direct contact by salesperson
- direct mail

However, there are two main ways in which they might also be attracted as a result of the operations function. These are:

- word of mouth (i.e., hearing about the product from friends)
- previous purchase with which they are satisfied

Both of these are based upon the experience that the customer had when they bought the product the first time. It is often said that it is very easy to sell something to someone *once*, but the great achievement lies in the repeat purchase.

Many people, when they think of attracting customers, immediately look to the marketing department. Often it is the marketing staff who receive all the training in customer relations to the neglect of operating staff.

One of the most important points about the TQM approach is that it lays the responsibility for achieving quality on all departments and allows them to focus on how they can serve the customer best.

Once the customer has tried the product, the response of the operations function is likely to be a crucial factor in their choice of whether they try it again.

In fact, if we look at the whole length of the relationship between organization and customer and show which function is likely to be in the closest contact with the customer, it would look something like that shown in figure 6.1.

In fact, the actual level of involvement will tend to vary according to the product, but this diagram is useful in stressing the fact that there is a very great involvement between the customer and operations staff, and organizations ignore this relationship at their peril.

THINK POINT

Consider your own organization. Who are the people who have most contact with the customer?

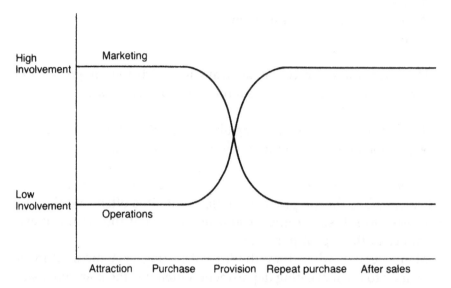

Figure 6.1 Marketing and operations, relationship with customer

In many cases the staff who are most in contact with the customer are those who are given least training to be able to cope with it. Let's think of a couple of examples:

- Part-time bar staff taken on in a busy pub
- Saturday morning sales staff at a High Street shop

Remember, it is rarely the managing director or the chairman who meets your customers, so it is necessary to ensure that if you have staff responsible to you who regularly meet the customer they receive the appropriate training to allow them to respond in the correct manner.

In the first chapter of this volume we saw that there are both internal and external customers, and it is very likely that you may have both. The same principles apply to both types of customer. Just because someone works in the same organization does not mean that you can treat them differently. They require the same standards of workmanship, the same civility and respect, and the same urgency. After all, somewhere at the end of the chain of internal customers is an external customer on whose behalf they are acting.

Let's look at some examples of internal customers:

- A mechanic who wants a part from the stores
- A clerk who wants some stationery from the person in charge

- A person who is waiting for some information that you have for her
- A person collecting his wages from the pay clerk

So whenever you are doing any job for anyone else in your organization they should be considered as a customer and treated accordingly.

Now let's look at some of the reasons why communication takes place between the operations function and the customer:

1 General enquiries and information
2 Advising the customer of altered arrangements
3 Communication with customers who are queuing
4 Regular liaison
5 Feedback from customers

We shall look at each of these categories in turn.

GENERAL ENQUIRIES FOR INFORMATION

A customer may want further information about a product to:

- help him to choose which is the best for him
- check availability
- find out how the product works

For example, a businessman may need to attend a meeting the next day and wants to find out which is the most suitable train to take; or someone may ring up their local library to find out whether they usually stock a particular book; or a customer may not really understand the instructions concerning the product she has bought.

There are a number of ways that such requests can be received, including telephone, letter and fax; and verbally, in a face-to-face discussion.

Before we look at some of the important factors entailed in responding to such requests, we should ask ourselves whether, in fact, there was some way that we could have anticipated them. In our examples above:

- timetables could be distributed to local business users
- regular library users could be sent lists of new books taken into stock

- instructions could be more detailed or a demonstration might
  be given on purchase if the product is particularly complicated

When a request for information is received, the most important first step is to ensure that any response is given promptly.

We have already mentioned setting standards for response times to telephone calls. The same should apply to any other type of communication. In the case of letters, they can be stamped to show the date they were received, while faxes are timed and dated anyway. You may think that no standards should be necessary for face-to-face requests, but how often have you stood at a counter being ignored while staff carry on their conversation?

If it is not possible to give an immediate answer, then a holding response should be given. However, there is a great danger here that once the initial response has been made within the standard laid down, the follow-up never occurs.

There are many instances that can be mentioned, but the classic and most common is the promise that you will ring back later. What usually happens is that the customer's request needs further research or consultation with another party (such as one of your suppliers); you have not yourself received any response, so there is nothing to tell the customer. However, there is something that you can tell the customer: you can tell them that you are not yet in a position to answer but that you are still trying and will contact them again when you have something more. Then say when you expect that to be.

When giving a response it is vital that any information passed to the customer is accurate and up to date. In chapter 4 we looked at ensuring that procedural manuals and amendments were up to date. The same applies to any publications which are used in communication with customers. This means that when you do send them information, such as timetables etc., you must ensure that they are on the mailing list for any subsequent amendments that might be issued. This should also be taken into account when the costs of issuing such information are being considered. If the cost of updating is going to prove too much, then it may well be better not to issue them in the first place.

It is important that any staff who give information to customers are supported by adequate training in respect of the products concerned. It can be very irritating if staff appear to know even less than the customer. Numerous examples can be found anywhere along the

High Street, from stores selling electrical goods to travel agents, where it is quite apparent that the level of knowledge is not high.

It is a fine judgement as to when a member of staff should be allowed to give information on their own, as it is impossible for one person to have a complete fund of knowledge. In any case, experience gained in the job is likely to improve both their knowledge and their ability to communicate with customers. It is important, however, that they are given a basic product knowledge together with the knowledge of where to find out something that they do not know.

However irrational it may seem, the customer expects employees to know a lot about the organization they work for, and will be unimpressed if the employee gives the appearance of not knowing or, even worse, not caring. Some of the most common failings that can lead to customer dissatisfaction are:

- Telephoning a switchboard and being told that they have never heard of the person to whom you wish to speak. A list of departments and extension numbers provided for the switchboard operator would prevent this from happening.
- Asking in a supermarket where a particular item can be found and receiving the response 'I don't know, I've just started here'. A properly trained member of staff would either know or offer to find out (and because they had been told where to obtain information they would know how to set about finding it).
- Requesting a particular item and being told 'I'm sorry, we don't have any', when it is clearly visible on the shelf if the employee could be bothered to turn around and look.

Often, customers want advice about a particular product. It is important that any advice given is within the competence of the person who is giving it. If a client asks a particularly detailed question about a particular holiday destination which requires local experience to answer, then it would be unwise for the travel consultant who had never been there to try to give a generalized response. Much better to give a holding response and carry out further research.

Similarly, people take cameras into shops that sell film and ask the assistant if they can load it for them. They may not have the necessary knowledge to do so and damage the camera instead.

It is best to remember that if advice turns sour the organization may end up facing a claim for compensation to which it will have little defence.

Advice should be given by a person only if they have the necessary knowledge, experience and training to do so.

Otherwise, either further advice should be sought from someone else in the organization who has the necessary knowledge, or, if there is no one, the customer should be advised to consult an appropriate expert.

ADVISING THE CUSTOMER OF ALTERED ARRANGEMENTS

There are occasions when it is necessary to change the arrangements that have been advertised or which have been agreed with customers. We saw earlier, when we looked at short-term planning, that it is helpful to have a list of people to inform when plans are changed. One of the most important of these will be the customer. Depending upon the situation, there are a number of ways that contact can be made:

1 If there is time, a letter will sometimes be sufficient. The problem here is that it may not allow the client enough time or opportunity to comment on the revised plan, nor does it give them any opportunity to be consulted. For example, a consignment of nuts and bolts were to have been delivered in a week's time on a Thursday, but it turns out that they will not be ready to go out until the following Monday. A letter informing the customer of this new arrangement may solve the supplier's problems, but might be totally unacceptable to the customer who wanted to use them over the intervening week-end. By the time the letter is received and acted upon, the supplier's plans may be too far advanced to change and a potential conflict with the customer would appear to be inevitable.

2 On the other hand, a telephone call to negotiate new arrangements to ensure that they were suitable would avoid such conflict: the compromise of a Friday delivery might be acceptable to both parties.

Of course, failure to advise the client at all of any new arrangements is likely to jeopardize not only the current order, but also any future orders that may be available.

Any of the usual methods of communication may be used, but some additional aids are used in some industries, such as transport, public address systems, television screens and computerized departure and arrival boards. When all are used together, as they often are at airports, they can be a very powerful means of communication. They allow passengers to be kept fully informed about the flight they may be intending to catch or meet.

One of the factors to be borne in mind here is that if flights are shown as being delayed and time is subsequently made up – for example, by bringing the next service forward – it is important that the new arrangements are broadcast widely, especially in the restaurants and cafes where passengers may have gone to while away the time. There is nothing quite so frustrating for them as having to watch their retimed flight depart as they gaze out of the restaurant window!

While customers may well be put out by any revisions of plans, they are much more likely to be understanding if they are told the reason for them. Once they realize that there has been a machine breakdown and you simply have not been able to make up their order, they are more likely to accept the situation than if they feel you may have given someone else priority. Similarly, passengers sitting in an aeroplane waiting for a take-off slot will feel less frustrated if they are told about the situation and given some revised estimate of take-off.

In an earlier chapter we mentioned contingency plans. Any customers who are likely to be affected by bringing these into operation should be included in the plan. Emergency services usually have contingency plans to deal with major problems, such as a huge leak of toxic gas. Included in these plans will be methods to be used to inform the people affected, including television and radio announcements. In the nuclear disaster at Chernobyl in the Ukraine little thought was given to this particular aspect.

COMMUNICATION WITH CUSTOMERS IN THE QUEUE

We saw in chapter 3 that queuing was a very common method of managing capacity. Most people are prepared to accept an element of queuing in certain situations. We also mentioned that they could be in a queue

- in the shop or store
- on the telephone
- at home or at their work premises

It is very important that contact and communication is maintained while people are queuing, especially if it is expected to last a long time.

In a supermarket or a bank, the opening of another checkout or window reassures waiting customers that the organization is aware that they are having to wait longer than usual. If it is not possible to do this because of a shortage of staff, then a notice to that effect will at least inform customers of the reason for the longer wait and assure them that their situation is not simply being ignored.

Telephone queuing is rather more difficult. Recorded holding messages informing the client that they will be answered as soon as possible if they would like to hold on are not popular with everyone. To begin with, once the phone is answered by the automatic recording the customer is involved in the cost of the phone call. Therefore, if it is necessary to use such a system (and it often is), the choice of the answering message will be crucial.

Automatic responses vary and might include the following:

- A short message explaining that the client will be answered in rotation, repeated at intervals with nothing in between
- The same as above with details of some of the products of the organization given in between
- Music played in between. Should this method be used the choice of what type to play may be crucial. Whichever type is selected will convey something about the organization to the client.

The most effective system is to ensure that all calls are answered within a target period to avoid potential customers being lost. This will involve decisions being made about the number of telephone lines and the number of staff needed to achieve the target. Computer measuring equipment to give information in this respect is available and its use is becoming more and more common.

Clients waiting at home or at their places of work need to be kept informed of progress too. For example, if a furniture store knows when it is likely to be able to deliver the three piece suite that was ordered, a card sent to the customer advising them of the suggested date and asking them to confirm whether it is convenient is both cheap and effective. Should the order not be progressing as expected, then the client should be advised accordingly so that they have an opportunity of making any necessary alterations to their plans: they may well have agreed to sell their old suite on the same day that the new one was expected, and advice of delay will allow them to hold on to it a little longer.

A patient waiting on a long list for a hospital operation should be advised from time to time of the current situation so that they are reassured that they have not been forgotten.

We have already considered the situation of the firm awaiting delivery of nuts and bolts, and how important it is to keep it advised of progress.

REGULAR LIAISON

Regular liaison between supplier and client can take two forms: formal and informal.

Formal liaison

Formal contact would include any regular meetings where minutes might be produced. Where there is a very close working relationship between the parties there may be a quarterly or even a monthly formal meeting, depending upon the complexity of the product and the degree of contact that is felt to be necessary.

Discussions might cover areas such as:

- contracts
- progress on projects
- design problems
- joint cooperation
- future opportunities

In some instances, such as the current and former nationalized industries, consumers are represented by an official body who carries on this formal liaison role on their behalf. These bodies include OFTEL (telephones) and TUCC (transport).

Informal liaison

Informal liaison covers a whole range of activities including:

- *ad hoc* meetings and visits
- regular telephone and fax contact

- continuous contact in cases where the customer has a permanent presence in the supplier's premises: for example, when collaborating on product design to meet the customer's exact requirements
- exchange of Christmas cards and calendars
- meetings over lunch
- sending clients in-house newsletters or newspapers

Regular liaison will help to identify potential problems before they arise, or at least to recognize them as soon as they do. Shared solutions are likely to cement relationships between supplier and client, and once a bond of loyalty is developed this can be a very powerful factor in the battle against any competition that arises.

FEEDBACK FROM CUSTOMERS

We talked in chapter 5 about the need to make a distinction between things going according to plan and success being achieved. If the plan itself is not the correct one to achieve this success, then it needs to be changed. How do we know whether we have the right plan?

Our customers will let us know in the following ways:

- if they are satisfied, they will buy the product in the amounts we predicted in our sales forecasts; if not, they will buy elsewhere
- they will give direct feedback on elements of the product.

Let's look in more detail at how we might obtain from the customer feedback which is likely to be of enormous benefit to us. We saw in figure 3.1 the importance of obtaining feedback, and this is especially so in the case of feedback from customers. Depending upon how much we want to spend, there are a number of ways we can achieve this:

- Face-to-face surveys using specialist companies to obtain reaction to the products through carefully structured questions. This can be carried out in the high street or on the premises of the organization.
- Telephone surveys might be used in the same way.
- Where there is a longer relationship between customer and

organization, feedback is likely to be one of the subjects of regular liaison that we mentioned earlier in this chapter.

- In the case of local councils, the customers are given the opportunity for feedback at regular elections.
- Customer suggestions and feedback forms are a relatively inexpensive method of obtaining feedback. Many shops have books where the customer is invited to make any suggestions for improvements. In hotels, there is usually a specially designed form which asks a number of specific questions about the service received. There is often a guest diary in which the clients are invited to make any comments about how well they enjoyed their stay, and to give advice to future guests that they feel may be useful. Other organizations write to their customers and invite comments.

Customer complaints are another very useful source of feedback. Let's look at them in more detail.

CUSTOMER COMPLAINTS

The number of customer complaints that an organization receives is a very small fraction of the actual complaints that it might receive, because most people do not complain. The percentage of people who actually complain compared with people who are dissatisfied with some particular aspect of a product will vary according to a number of factors:

- the price paid (the higher the price the more likely a dissatisfied customer will be to complain)
- the importance of the product to the customer (if it is a vital engineering part, say, or if the product was bought as a present for someone)
- the expectations of the customer (if they expected a pair of shoes to last longer)
- the background of the customer (Americans are much less likely to accept poor service than the British, for example)
- other experiences that the customer has had (if complaints in a particular industry have been ignored before, or if the factor causing dissatisfaction is so prevalent that they would be complaining all of the time, then they might not bother)

- the amount of hassle they feel will be involved (it takes more effort to write a letter than to fill in a form, while it may cause embarrassment to some customers if they complain in a restaurant: they may even lie and say they enjoyed a meal when they did not)

In some organizations, one of the ways that the level of service is judged is by the increase or decrease in the number of complaints received. This may be mathematically acceptable in that the fewer dissatisfied customers there are then the fewer will be the number of people who actually complain, and vice versa.

However, this kind of approach may lead the organization to make it harder for the customer to complain, which means that the figures relate only to the hard core of people who are determined that they want their complaint to be heard. Such an approach may also lead to an attitude according to which the organization does not want to hear about anything that is going wrong because it may make the figures look bad. This is the ostrich approach: the organization believes that what it does not see while its head is buried in the sand will not hurt it! Meanwhile customers drift away to its competitors.

A successful organization will want to know when its service falls short of what is expected so that it can do something about it. This is the eagle approach, which involves being ever on the lookout for things that may be causing customers to drift away to the competition.

If we consider that most people who are dissatisfied do not bother to complain, but simply do not buy the product again, what are the implications?

Let's consider what a complaint offers the organization that a shrug of resignation by the customer does not.

- The complaint represents an opportunity. Most people who complain actively want to give the organization another chance. It is as if the customer were saying 'I know you got it wrong this time but perhaps you can do better next time'.
- The resigned shrug says 'You got it wrong this time and you won't get the chance to get it wrong again'.

The complaint also gives us:

- Information about the product. It shows where we are going wrong and why customers might not be buying it. Consider how much it would cost to purchase such information from a specialist survey company. Here the customer is offering it free of charge.

- An opportunity to put things right, either by replacing the product or by taking action immediately to prevent things deteriorating further. A tour operator might offer another room to a client who is dissatisfied with the one she has been allocated.
- A chance to offer compensation when the case demands it.
- The possibility of recovering the situation to such an extent that the customer moves from a position of dissatisfaction to one of satisfaction. They may even begin to recommend the organization to their friends again by stressing the excellent way in which it dealt with their complaint.

So how should we deal with a complaint? Well, let's look at our objectives.

- We want to turn a dissatisfied customer back into a satisfied customer as far as that is possible.
- We also want to find out what has gone wrong and put it right.

First, it is important to realize that whatever happened was the customer's experience and they own it. Whatever our feelings about the matter, we cannot deny how the customer feels. We may think that the meal seems all right, but if the customer is not enjoying it he is unlikely to come back to the restaurant again. Proving that the steak is fine is unlikely to make him enjoy it any more.

So whether or not the complaint being made is wholly the organization's fault is not the issue. The important thing is how the client feels.

One of the strongest factors in the favour of Marks and Spencer is their returns policy. There is no hassle, because if the customer is dissatisfied in any way then it can be returned, even if it was their fault for buying the wrong size in the first place. It is as simple as that.

When dealing with a complaint, whether written or verbal, the tone of the response is very important. An offhand reply is unlikely to succeed, so politeness at all times is important, even if the client is angry.

A prompt reply is also vital, for if the response is early enough further deterioration in the situation may be prevented and the recovery may be a lot easier. Where the occurrence is in the past, a prompt reply at least encourages the client that his feelings are valued and that the complaint is being taken seriously.

A positive response is preferable in most situations. This may mean exchanging a product, offering compensation or acting in some other way to show that the client is important.

THINK POINT

Let's look at some examples of complaints that might be received. How would you deal with them?

- A customer returns a garment because the stitching has come undone. It has clearly been worn.
- A hamburger is returned because it has mayonnaise on it which the customer does not like. All of the pictures around the restaurant show hamburgers with salad and mayonnaise on them.
- A major customer has returned a whole batch of nuts and bolts which were specially made for him. It seems that he inadvertently gave you the wrong specification.
- An angry customer is complaining that her hotel room is very small and cramped when the brochure distinctly described them as spacious.

There is no one right answer in any of these cases. However, let's look at some of the implications of these complaints.

The returned garment may well have been worn and the stitching may have come away as a result of some mistreatment. However, can you be sure of this? And in any case the garment should be expected to survive normal wear and tear. How long ago it was purchased may have a bearing on the situation. One thing it may allow you to do is to investigate whether there have been any similar problems with that particular batch. You may well find that faulty garments are being produced at this very moment which you can now take action to prevent.

Just because the pictures of the hamburgers show mayonnaise on all of them, can you be sure that the customer was aware of this? Put yourself in her place. Would you have ordered it if you had known? Clearly, you need to reconsider whether the menu is sufficiently clear. You might also have identified a need for a hamburger with no mayonnaise at all. You could then consider whether your production systems are flexible enough for one to be made at an acceptable cost. If some compensation is not made it is unlikely that this customer will use the restaurant again. On the other hand, a special hamburger made for her followed by a change of menu might secure her loyalty (and that of her friends) for the future.

The incorrect sizes of the nuts and bolts were clearly the customer's fault. However, are you satisfied that you give as much advice to customers as they might need? Perhaps there is a case for looking at this aspect of the service for the future. As a gesture of goodwill you might refund to the customer's account any scrap value you receive for the nuts and bolts, or, if you can subsequently resell them, the full value. How you dealt with this may well be decided by the value of future orders, compared with which this particular order might be trivial. You might even feel it is worth bearing the cost yourself.

The angry hotel room occupant certainly seems to be justified in her complaint. You need to find out why she has been given a room which clearly contravenes the claims made in your brochure. What about the other people on the tour, what kind of rooms have they been allocated? This complaint may only be one of many about to arise. She should be moved to another room immediately, preferably a particularly attractive one to compensate her for the inconvenience already caused. You might also like to consider making some kind of goodwill gesture, such as a complimentary bottle of wine at dinner or a complimentary excursion to make up for her initial disappointment.

If you have dealt with a complaint successfully, you will have satisfied the earlier objectives that were set.

You will have used the second chance that the customer has given you and used it as a sales opportunity to ensure that they buy from you again.

You will have checked any possible failures that might have occurred and rectified any problems found.

Where a customer has brought to light a particular situation that has enabled you to prevent future problems, a letter of thanks and some other goodwill gesture should certainly be considered.

This policy of looking positively at complaints fits in well with the TQM approach of finding solutions to problems before they happen.

Now, let's take another visit to our hotel.

Case Note 12

Elaine was looking forward to the next disco because it would give her the opportunity to show that she could get it right. However, one of her main concerns was that very few people might turn up after the problems at the last one. This would be ironic, as most of the original problems stemmed from the fact that more people turned up than were expected.

She was particularly concerned about people like Julie, the customer she had overheard saying that whe was never going to come back again even for a drink. If she lost people like her and her friends the disco would turn out to have affected the future of the hotel adversely rather than in the positive way that she had hoped.

However, she had had an enormous stroke of good fortune. She was sitting in her office when Julie knocked at the door. Apparently, she had lost her umbrella and she thought it might have been at the hotel on the evening of the disco. She had come to see if it had been found.

Elaine asked Jane, the waitress, to go and find out whether it had been handed in. While they awaited her return, Elaine thought she would try to recover the situation with Julie. She explained what she had felt had gone wrong and what she intended to do to prevent the problems arising again. She could see that Julie was sympathetic to her honesty.

Finally, she promised that if she and her friends were to attend she would give them each a voucher for a free bottle of wine between two next time either they used the restaurant or took a bar meal in the leisure complex. She mentally calculated that there were about twenty of them in the group and this would cost the company some ten bottles of wine if they took up the offer.

Julie thought about it for a moment and then, with a smile, she said, 'OK, we'll give it one more try'. At that moment Jane came back with her umbrella.

Elaine has possibly rectified the situation now, at least with this particular group of people. Once word gets around that they are coming again, then the numbers should remain sufficiently large. She breathed a sigh of relief. Then she thought about the free bottles of wine. In order to qualify for them Julie and her friends would all have to come into the hotel for a meal, either at the restaurant or, more likely, the leisure complex. Either way they would have to spend more money. Then if they liked it they might start to come here to eat regularly. A disaster would then have turned into a triumph.

One other important part of customer communication is after-sales service.

AFTER-SALES SERVICE

This is often one of the features that are stressed during the marketing process. There are various types of after-sales service:

- Repairs of faults that occur within the guarantee period. This should be made as easy as possible for the customer. Where the fault occurs very shortly after purchase, consideration should be given to replacing the product rather than repairing.
- Exchange of faulty goods. Unused goods which are faulty should be exchanged. The situation should also be referred to the manufacturer in case there is an inherent fault running through a whole batch. Compensation for services which are not performed satisfactorily should also be given. Many travel companies already produce a scale of compensation that will be paid in the event that the intended service is not fully provided.
- Repairs carried out after the expiry of the guarantee (often carried out under service agreements by third parties). Full details of the arrangements should, where possible, be given at the time of purchase. Many companies selling video recorders and televisions offer an extended warranty deal at additional cost so that customers who take up the offer are protected after the initial guarantee runs out.
- Updating customers on new products that might be useful. Many customers who purchase items are interested in products that are associated with them. Buyers of computers may well be glad to receive literature on the programs available for them. Where possible, the customer's attitude to this should be established at the time of purchase by including a card that allows them to register on a mailing list. Many companies now operate a system where the customer is automatically sent information unless they fill in a card to say that they do not want it. The approach will depend upon the industry concerned and the ethics of the organization. However, it is as

well to be aware that some customers object to the latter approach and regard it as a misuse of personal information.

- Service calls to ensure that everything is working correctly. This will be part of the regular liaison where a long-term relationship exists with the customer. This is also likely to form part of the service call made by sales representatives. It may not be the reason for the salesperson's call, but the customer is certain to bring the matter up if there are any problems.
- Networking between the organization and customers. Some organizations invite clients to special promotional evenings such as:
  - wine tastings
  - fine art previews or exhibitions
- Or they may make special offers to previous clients such as:
  - reducing the price of a car service
  - frequent flier schemes run by a number of airlines, in which the more often the airline is used, the more free travel is earned

The result of these types of offer is that the customer feels valued and develops a strong loyalty to the product or organization. Both are likely to be considered as part of the company's marketing strategy.

Another important aspect of customer communications is the concept of front line and behind the scenes staff.

FRONT LINE AND BEHIND THE SCENES

Front line staff work with the customer and are highly 'visible', while back room staff are rarely seen.

Front line staff do not actually have to be seen: a telephone operator would certainly be front line because of the contact with the customer. Back room staff, on the other hand, may be be seen, as through the indoor glass of banks and building societies, but have little contact with clients and act in a supporting role to the front line staff.

In a TQM approach, it would be important that quality issues were applied to both front line and back room staff. A well arranged and tidy filing cabinet would be as important as an immaculate serving position. The appearance of staff in either position would be expected to be exemplary.

When failures occur behind the scenes they can be just as spectacular as those in the front line. Live television broadcasters often relax when they are off camera. Should a technician leave the camera or microphone on while this is happening then the results are often as unexpected as they can be embarrassing. If the same standards were applied to both situations then there would be little chance of this happening.

The amount of behind-the-scenes staff that the organization employs is often used as a marketing ploy. Some stress that costs are kept low because there is no costly administration for the customer to pay for. Companies using direct mail often claim to cut down the costs because they are cutting out the retail operator. Many customers, especially if they know what they want already and do not need any further advice, find this approach attractive.

Others emphasize the fact that the customer is so special that they need a lot of looking after and that staff will be available to ensure that they are. Examples of this are:

- twenty-four-hour room service at hotels
- fully escorted tours in foreign countries
- the low staff/client ratio claimed by some deluxe hotels or cruise ships
- the large range of service outlets offered by some manufacturing companies.

Many organizations are involved in programmes to ensure that their staff, whether front line or behind the scenes, recognize the importance of the customer.

PUTTING THE CUSTOMER FIRST

We have seen that it is necessary that this should be a total approach, and that everyone (not just front line staff who are meeting the customer) should be involved in such schemes if they are to be effective. After all, a person requiring information is likely to ask anyone that they think is connected to the firm, whether they are behind the counter or walking across an airport concourse, especially if the member of staff is in uniform.

Often it is the experience that the client gains from people who do not usually meet the customer that governs his or her attitude to the whole company. This may be equally true in the case of a sub-contractor: a passenger may well assume that the subcontractor cleaning the travel centre windows is a member of the railway station staff. A reply of 'How should I know?' to the request for information as to which platform he might go to in order to catch the London train, may well produce a complaint against station staff. The passenger may well travel by coach next time.

TQM and customer first programmes, therefore, should not be confined to staff of the organization. They should be extended to include subcontractors and suppliers.

The 'putting the customer first approach' often involves a change in the company culture. As such, it has to be supported through all levels of management, otherwise it is likely to fail.

The approach is not only confined to such issues as total quality and 'politeness at all times', but may sometimes affect some of the fundamental conditions of service of the staff involved. For example, many staff in a number of industries receive perks as part of their salary structure. Often these perks include free enjoyment of a certain amount of goods or services, such as:

- free travel
- free accommodation
- free use of cars
- free meals
- free manufactured items

Putting the customer first may well mean that the staff have to forgo some of these perks, at least at peak times. This may produce a conflict between the needs of the customer and the entitlements of the staff.

In addition, staff may well view such programmes as 'just another fad' that won't last. This is especially likely if similar schemes have been tried unsuccessfully in the past. If they feel this, they will not put in sufficient effort to make it work.

In order for the programmes to be successful, they need total commitment from all staff and levels of management, and they need to be applied throughout the organization.

SUMMARY

Supervisory Management Standards:

Unit 1   Maintain services and operations to meet quality standards

Element 1.1 Maintain services and operations

         1.2 Maintain the necessary conditions for an effective and safe environment

Unit 2   Contribute to the planning, monitoring and control of resources

Element 2.1 Plan for the use of resources

         2.2 Monitor and control the use of resources

Unit 5   Contribute to the planning, organization and evaluation of work

Element 5.1 Contribute to planning work activities and methods to achieve objectives

         5.2 Organize work and assist in the evaluation of work

---

Communication with the customer is an activity which should be considered as fundamental to the whole organization.

The operations function has a major part to play in this communication.

We have looked at a number of ways that organizations and their customers communicate.

Communication should be a two-way process.

Putting the customer first is a total approach which must be embraced by the whole organization and in some cases its suppliers.

Chapter 7
Managing Materials

Supervisory Management Standards:

Unit 2   Contribute to the planning, monitoring and control
              of resources
Element 2.1 Plan for the use of resources
        2.2 Monitor and control the use of resources

Within the management standards for supervisors there are no criteria that relate specifically to the managing of materials. They relate to the managing of resources (elements 2.1 and 2.2), of which materials is only one part, as we discovered in our analysis of the operations process in chapters 2 and 4. However, the management of materials is so important to the operations process that a whole chapter needs to be devoted to it. Relationships with suppliers are also an important issue and the standards require that evidence be produced to demonstrate that care is taken to establish good working arrangements with them.

Managing materials is also known as **inventory management**. Let's look and see what we mean by inventory. The term is used to cover all forms of material that may be used by the organization and includes:

- raw materials
- finished goods used as an input to the operations process
- materials used for maintenance
- spares
- partly finished work (work in progress)
- items used in administration (such as stationery)
- finished stock ready for distribution to the customer

Inventory has been called 'the root of all evil' by one Japanese manager. Japanese manufacturing companies have been in the fore-front of the trend towards reducing the amount of inventory that is held. They view it as both an unnecessary cost that has to be borne and also as an encouragement towards inefficiency. This is because there is a tendency in most people to be rather wasteful of materials when they appear to be in an abundant supply. Scarce resources are usually treated more carefully.

We only need to look at the use of stationery. If there are unlimited supplies of paper or pens, for example, people will take more than they need. They lose the pens or throw them away before they are fully used up, while they use good quality paper for rough work, throwing most of it away into the wastepaper bin.

If the same items are more carefully controlled, then the pens last longer and scrap paper will be used for rough work. Many people who leave a large organization to start up their own business are shocked by the costs of stationery. They quickly adjust to the necessity for controlling its use!

There are a number of costs incurred by holding inventory, and these include:

- managerial time and effort to ensure that they are used as efficiently as possible
- storage costs, which include the costs of installing racks and bins to hold the items, and any special arrangements that are necessary for dangerous goods
- handling costs, both inwards and outwards, including the costs of recording and issuing them for use
- warehouse costs, such as rent or the loss of use of the area for other activities
- security provisions, which range from the installation of fences and compounds to security cameras or, in very large organizations, the services of specialist security staff
- investment opportunities are lost because the money is tied up in stock
- wastage, as we considered earlier: people are less careful when supplies are plentiful
- damage, since the longer an item is stored the more chance of damage being incurred
- insurance costs, especially for high value items such as TV sets or video recorders
- obsolescence, as many items quickly become outdated, either because they are perishable or because new versions constantly become available; with some dangerous goods, additional costs are incurred by the need to dispose of the

obsolescent items safely in accordance with the codified procedures. It is important that whenever new items arrive the stock already on hand is used up first. A clear method to ensure that this rotation of stock is carried out should be implemented.

THINK POINT

What is the attitude of your staff towards some common items of inventory, such as stationery? Do you feel that there is sufficient realization of the costs involved? What improvements can you make?

Some of the measures you might consider are:

- recycling scrap paper for use in rough work
- supplying expensive items on a shared basis rather than individually
- itemizing the cost of some of the items used and circularizing them to your staff
- setting a target for expenditure and trying to stick to it

So there are good reasons for reducing the amount of inventory held by an organization. Japanese manufacturers have pioneered the use of 'just in time' systems which achieve this particular aim. We will look at them in more detail later in this chapter.

In Britain, the attitude towards inventories was very relaxed until the late 1970s. Before that, many organizations had very poor control over the amount of inventory they held. If a member of staff needed six items, this would often be scaled up to ten to guard against the possibility of:

- all requests being scaled down
- some items being defective
- more than six being needed

In addition, there was little control of items within the organization. Shops could only guess at the stock they were carrying; no one really knew for certain.

During the recession of the late 1970s organizations were forced to look at new ways to reduce their costs in order to remain competitive. Inventory offered enormous scope for action. Computer systems offering management information became increasingly important, allowing companies to be aware of exactly what stock they were carrying.

It soon became clear that it was not necessary to hold such huge amounts of stock. If inventory was managed properly, the person needing six items would only need to order six and not ten, because he would know immediately whether his request could be met or not. His order could also be checked by other people so that it would become clear whether he was overordering or not. More attention was paid to quality, and in any case it was easier to check the smaller inventory, so there was less likelihood of there being any defective items. At the same time, if he found he needed more he could quickly find out where they were available.

The realization of the true cost of holding inventory and the reductions that could be achieved spawned a huge new industry, the premium transport operator. Previously, because companies held such large stocks, parcels carriers were able to take four to five days to deliver. Now that such large stocks were not being held, this was no longer acceptable. Delivery was needed overnight or even the same day. British Rail's 'Red Star' service was the pioneer, but many other competitors like TNT joined in.

Other kinds of specialist companies were able to thrive because they would provide an item through the premium carrier or by their own transport at very short notice, eliminating the need for the organization to hold the item itself. An example of this would be pumping equipment. Instead of buying it themselves and using it rarely, companies would simply hire it in at short notice when they needed it.

Since then the trend has continued and inventory management is seen as a crucial factor in the control of costs in any organization.

There are, however, some very good reasons for maintaining inventory too. Let's look at some good reasons for maintaining stocks of the various types of inventory that we mentioned at the beginning of the chapter.

Reasons for keeping inventories of raw materials (including finished goods used as inputs):

- To ensure consistency of supply, especially where it is known that there might be shortages

- The purchase of seasonal goods as they become available
- Taking advantage of suppliers' discounts
- Anticipating a price increase

Maintenance items and spares:

- To allow a quick restoration of the system in the event of a breakdown. The amount and type of spares carried will depend upon a number of factors, such as:

  - How quickly spares can be obtained
  - How important the item is to the operating process
  - The cost of the item

- To allow preventative maintenance to be carried out, thereby reducing the likelihood of a breakdown. Most organizations have a programme of maintenance for their machinery with the aim of reducing the amount of time that it is out of service. We will look at maintenance in more detail in the next chapter

Partly finished work:

- Working on different parts of the product at different locations within the workplace allows great flexibility. We looked at batch systems in chapter 2. Work in progress is usually found in manufacturing systems, but it can also be found in service industries. The meat stock made by Marc, the chef, which will be used for soups and gravies, could be considered as partly finished work.

Items used in administration:

- Clearly there needs to be a stock of stationery items or the administrative systems will grind to a halt. It is particularly prone to both wastage and pilfering, however, and is often difficult to control.

Finished goods:

- Customers are more likely to buy the product if they can see it in stock. Impulse buying will only occur if the product can be seen.
- The product can be made immediately available to customers

without them having to wait. This may give the company the edge over the competition and might be part of a total quality package being offered. Finished stock may also be applied to intangible items such as package tours. Tour operators hold a stock of holidays for which they may already have paid their suppliers. Failure to have them available on demand would almost inevitably mean a loss of business to the competition.

- To provide a steady, average supply of stock where demand is not constant. We looked at the process of smoothing to cope with capacity problems in chapter 3. The additional costs of holding the extra inventory may be more than offset by the savings made by setting production at a constant level.
- To meet a seasonal demand. Stocks are usually built up in the High Street stores in the period before Christmas. It is sometimes possible to extend the season. Christmas, for example, seems to come earlier each year.
- To provide against a breakdown in the production process. Again, this will avoid customer disappointment. 'Just in time' systems (which we will look at later) do not follow this particular path.

The amount of stock held in each of these areas will be decided by the organization after calculating the amount of risk that exists in respect of each factor.

Generally speaking, different departments within the company have different viewpoints on the holding of inventory.

The table below (adapted from T. Hill, *Production/Operations Management*, by permission of Prentice Hall) shows the levels of inventory which tend to be preferred by the various departments.

	Finance	*Operations*	*Sales*
Raw materials	low	high	not important
Work in prog.	low	high	not important
Maintenance	low	high	not important
Finished stock	low	low	high

It should be noted that from the finance department's point of view inventory is merely an additional cost in all cases. Operations tend to want stock available to give them maximum flexibility in the production process, while they want finished goods kept to a minimum because they lead to problems of storage and handling which we mentioned earlier. The sales department are only interested in finished goods being available for the customer at all times.

One concept which is useful when considering the costs of inventory is that of the **true cost of ownership** of a particular item. This takes into account all of the costs that are associated with it, including:

- special handling or storage costs
- administration, such as including it in a manual
- disposal costs after it has been used or become outdated
- delivery
- any training requirements
- percentage of material wasted

This helps to focus on the true cost rather than on just the first price you pay when you buy it.

One way of reducing the amount of inventory is to aim for as much standardization as possible. Let's consider the advantages and disadvantages.

STANDARDIZATION

Standardization involves having as small a range of designs as possible. The model T Ford was offered in only one colour, black. This subject brings into focus one of the continual tensions that exist between the marketing and operations departments. The marketing people want to try to satisfy the exact needs of each customer, which may be slightly different in each case, while the operations function wants the economies of scale that are obtainable by producing large numbers of essentially the same product.

Consider an airline which forecasts that there will be a potential demand for some thousand passengers per day between two points. Operationally, this could be achieved by the use of three flights each taking some three-hundred-odd passengers. This is attractive from many operational points of view, not least of which is the fact that only one type of aircraft is needed, with all of the implications that standardization offers in the way of training, materials, spares etc. However, this does not take into account the needs of the customer. There may be a demand throughout the day, so that a flight is needed at six different times. The different times may also be associated with different demands, so that while one flight might need an aeroplane to take three hundred passengers, the other five flights may only need an average of one hundred and forty seats each, thus requiring a totally different aeroplane. The actual solution will depend upon a number of factors, including such considerations as whether the range of choices required by the customer can actually be provided at an acceptable cost to the company.

The result of the marketing/operations conflict is often a compromise in which the overall most cost-effective solution is obtained, with some items being made to standard designs with others tailor-made. In fact, the tailor is a good example because the customer can usually buy off the peg or have suits made to measure.

When considering materials management, one of the best ways of overcoming the problem is to have a small number of basic designs, which form the core of the product, with a range of extras. This allows different end products to be offered.

Cars, for example, often have the same basic engines with different bodies, such as estates or hatchbacks. While in a travel agents you will find basic package holidays with a number of different add-on features.

This allows economies of scale to be achieved while maintaining a good selection of products for the customer. It has to be remembered that whenever a new piece of material is added to the process it comes complete with its 'true cost of ownership implications, including resetting of machines and corresponding retraining, while if it is used in small quantities it will probably cost more to either make or buy.

Now let's look at how we can plan to ensure the most effective use of materials.

MATERIALS PLANNING

One of the most important steps that a company can take is to adopt a culture which seeks to minimize the holding of inventory. This does not necessarily mean that it will not hold materials, but rather that it will always have a good reason when it does hold them.

It would not be good materials management for an arctic research station not to hold supplies if it receives an airlift only once a fortnight.

So the vital factor for a manager is that if materials are being held, they are being held for a good reason and in the correct quantities.

They should also be available in the appropriate quantities at the right time.

There are two types of items: dependent and independent.

Dependent items

The requirement for dependent items is, as the name implies, decided by the number of the final product that is needed. For example, if bicycles are being manufactured, then the number of wheels will depend upon the number of bicycles. Each bicycle will require:

- two wheels
- a frame
- a chain
- a set of gears
- pedals
- handlebars
- a saddle
- a front lamp bracket
- a rear lamp bracket etc.

So if we know the number of bicycles we require we can easily work out how many of each item we need. Forty bicycles will require eighty wheels, and so forth.

This is called a bill of materials. It is the final product exploded into its component parts.

Once we know how many we need, we have to decide when we want them. For example, we may need the frame, saddle and handlebars immediately because they are assembled during the first part of the process. However, the wheels may not be assembled until the following week, so if they were to be available at the same time as the frame, handlebars and saddle, they would simply lie around for a week doing nothing.

This does not necessarily mean that they are ordered a week later, because the important point is that they should be available for use during the next week, so the length of time they will take to arrive after being ordered (known as the 'lead time') will need to be taken into account. We will look in more detail at ordering and lead times later in the chapter.

The times when the various items are required for assembly and the dates that they need to be ordered to ensure their availability at the appropriate time are entered into a master schedule so that there is a clear picture of

- when items are being assembled in each week
- when they should be available
- when they should be ordered

As the items are used and new orders are received the master schedule is updated accordingly.

The number of the finished products required at any given time will depend upon the orders already in the pipeline, or the forecasts made by the marketing department of how many they estimate that they can sell. Many organizations are able to control their materials planning through the use of sophisticated computer systems.

Now let's see how all this affects Marc, our hotel chef.

He placed the order with his meat and fish suppliers several days ago and this would be delivered fresh during the morning before 11:00.

Let's look again at the menu Marc is planning for the private dinner party. Let's look at the starters first:

- Prawn cocktail 14
- Melon Surprise 4
- Bayonne Ham 2

Now let's first look at the amount of materials he needs:

- 2 oz of prawns for each cocktail means 28 oz of prawns. He uses a lot of prawns every day and usually buys them frozen in quantities of 2 lb bags. He usually carries at least a week's supply in the freezer, so all he needs to do is to defrost two bags on the day. There are plenty of bags left, enough for another two weeks, he reckons.
- Lettuce is a standard item in that it is also used in the salad for the vegetarian lasagne. These are bought fresh at the market in the morning, together with the vegetables.
- Prawn cocktail sauce is bought in large jars because they are cheaper. Marc notices that he will have enough for the party, but will need another jar soon.
- He needs half a melon for each person so will need to buy two at the market. They are filled with half a glass of white wine

each and two strawberries. He will need two glasses of wine from the cellar and will need eight strawberries. He will use the balance of the wine in the bottle in other courses.
- He needs eight slices of Bayonne ham fresh from the market.

Now let's look at the main courses:

- Roast Leg of Lamb 10
- Baked Trout 5
- Vegetable Lasagne 5

And the materials needed:

- The meat and fish orders had been placed several days ago to ensure that they would be available. These were arriving at 11:00. He estimated that he would need two large legs of lamb and five trout. His assistant would check that they were of top quality.
- The pasta for the lasagne was already in stock because it was bought in a bulk purchase, and the vegetables would be bought at the market.

THINK POINT

You might like to look at the materials requirements for the other courses.

As we have already mentioned, Japanese manufacturers have developed systems to reduce the need to hold inventory. They are known as **just in time** systems. As the name would suggest, such systems rely upon items becoming available at just the time that they are needed. Let's have a brief look and see how they work.

Just in time (JIT)

The main requirement for a JIT system is that the demand is both known and stable. The demand over the following period is agreed with customers and is then divided into a daily total so that the same number of items are manufactured each day. Each stage of the manufacturing process will only produce enough to satisfy the demand in the next stage. Once that situation has been reached, no further production will take place.

This is achieved by the use of a relatively simple system called **kanban** in Japanese companies, though the term is not always used in the UK. The true system is made up of containers and cards (production and withdrawal) and works as follows.

Let's assume that there are two work stations with station A producing material which will be used in station B. Let's also assume that there are six containers in use between them. Kanban cards, when they are in use, are the authority to produce material to fill another container and to move a full container to the next work station.

When B receives full containers of parts from A it will work on them until the containers are empty. As they are emptied the containers are taken back to station A, where they are loaded again and the process is repeated.

The process is controlled physically, in that work station A can only continue to fill containers when it receives empty ones back from B. A breakdown at either work station will lead to production being stopped at the other.

A breakdown at A would eventually be shown by a build-up of empty containers at A. Once all the containers were emptied by B and returned, then B would have to stop because of lack of material. A breakdown at B would be shown up by an accumulation of loaded containers at B, and A would have to stop because it would have no more containers to fill.

The factory floor in a JIT system is typified by a very orderly arrangement of containers located neatly at work stations.

There may well be a number of linked work stations producing parts for one or more subsequent machines.

At the very beginning of the process there is the receipt of material from the supplier. While in the usual materials planning systems there might be a warehouse where raw materials are received and stored, this is not the case with JIT. Instead, suppliers receive orders in small lots, or they may be sent empty containers to fill. They are expected to make frequent deliveries in order that inventory actually held is reduced as far as possible. Deliveries are often timed by the hour rather than the day or week as might be expected in other systems.

At the end of the JIT process, only the number required for the customer is produced each day so that there are no stocks of finished goods being stored. Should the customer not be able to accept then production will stop in the same way as mentioned earlier, because the containers at the last processing stage will be full, and there will be no more empty containers available to be filled. This in turn will stop all of the previous stages too.

There are several implications for organizations that wish to introduce such a system.

Firstly, quality is paramount. Any breakdown will have serious consequences on the whole production process. In other systems a breakdown can be overcome by using stocks already built up. Not so in JIT. This is often considered to be a bonus because it forces everyone involved to focus on quality, since even the slightest reduction in quality may cause the system to stop. This ensures that any problems that do occur are not simply glossed over but are considered at the highest management level. This may be contrasted with the attitude in some organizations, where the breakdown of equipment is not only tolerated but expected. In JIT, continual breakdowns would have a catastrophic effect.

Customers have to be involved in agreeing stable production targets. This usually leads to the building up of excellent relations and trust between customers and the company concerned.

Suppliers have to ensure that their working arrangements fit in perfectly with the JIT arrangements. This applies both to the actual delivery arrangements and to the quality specifications. There is no point in the company having all of its systems working perfectly if the material supplied does not meet the required standards. Clearly, there is a need for a quality check for all incoming material in much the same way as we mentioned in chapter 5. In fact it is easy to see why some Japanese companies aim for zero defects. Reliability of supply is also vital, as a failure of the supplier to provide materials will stop the whole process too.

With JIT systems it is rather impracticable to have a large number of suppliers, because of the need for them to work very closely with the company in a relationship of mutual trust. It might be considered that this would lead to higher prices being paid for supplies because of the inability to shop around for the best price. In fact the very opposite usually happens: this occurs because supplier and company work very closely together and as their experience of a particular process increases they are very likely to find new, more cost-effective methods, the savings from which both parties may well share.

There are also implications for the workforce. Machine operators may need to be trained on a number of processes in order to obtain maximum flexibility. Machines may have to be reset for new products quite often, and the time taken for this will have an effect on the productivity of the processes. Staff who can operate a number of systems quickly and effectively will reduce the time lost in this activity.

There are a number of companies in the UK which have introduced similar systems, though very few have gone as far as the Japanese. Many of the systems are actually hybrid, with the amount of inventory much reduced, often to about a week's supply of raw materials. Closer ties with suppliers are becoming much more common. A major car production plant, for example, may account for nearly all of a particular supplier's business. Trust is needed here as the supplier may feel very vulnerable in this situation.

What can happen is that an organization tries to introduce the JIT system where there are large variations in demand. The result is the need to reset machines for unexpected orders, leading to increased costs. Or they may find that the relationship with the supplier is not as close or trustworthy as they had expected and find themselves with no materials to input.

We have looked at the different ways in which dependent items might be managed. Now let's consider independent items.

Independent items

Independent items are those whose rate of utilization does not have a direct relationship with other items. The amount of sugar used in a café does not relate directly to the number of cups of tea and coffee sold. They are, therefore, independent items. An example from the hotel restaurant would be the salt and pepper. Vegetables might also be considered independent, unless the portions are strictly controlled so that the amount used is directly related to the number of meals served.

The very fact that items are independent means that we have to find ways of controlling them carefully, because otherwise we will not have any idea of how many we should buy at one time, nor of how many we should keep in stock.

Factors that we need to consider are:

- the number of items used over a specified period of time
- the time taken for an order to reach us once it has been ordered (the lead time)

- the space that is available for storage
- the cost of storage
- the cost of each separate order (for example, documentation or delivery charges)
- whether there are any discounts available for bulk purchases
- the risks associated with running out of a particular item

Once we have gathered this information we are in a position to consider the best way of controlling the items concerned.

Let's consider three ways: the periodic order, the economic order quantity, and the reorder point.

Periodic orders

The periodic order will apply when the supplier has a periodic system of delivery. The van is in our area at certain times only – for example, every Wednesday in the case of a supplier to a local shop. The order may be given in advance on an agreed day, which might be the Monday before. On the other hand, if it is known that the supplier will be carrying sufficient stock the order may well be given when the van arrives.

The order will take into account the number of items needed between now and the next delivery, less any that are already on hand.

If it is felt that there is a risk to the business if the stock of a particular item should run out, then a safety margin would be built in.

So a figure is reached of the amount of the item that should be on hand immediately after the delivery to allow the stock to last until the next delivery. This will be

- the number required before the next delivery
- plus any safety stock

The order will be that number less the number already on hand.

Let's see how this works out in practice.

The shop uses approximately fifteen cases of soft drinks per week, and the supplier calls on a weekly basis. The manager would not like to run out because his customers would go to the shop along the road and purchase their drinks there, so he likes to have at least three extra cases on hand as a safety stock. He has enough storage room for them. He still has some eight cases on hand when the supplier arrives.

THINK POINT

How many does the manager order?

The answer is ten cases.

He needs fifteen cases to satisfy the demand until next week. Add to this a further three cases as a safety stock to arrive at a figure of eighteen cases. The shop has eight cases of soft drinks on hand already, so this is deducted to leave an order of ten cases.

The periodic system, therefore, is based upon an amount that is required in order to ensure that the item lasts until the next delivery. This is of course very simplified, as it takes no account of seasonal variations. Clearly, during a hot spell the shop manager would increase his estimate of demand for drinks.

Figure 7.1 shows an example of a periodic order system in which orders are placed every week. It can be seen that in the first week the usual amount of fifteen cases were used, but only ten in week 2. In the third week, which was very busy, even the safety stock was sold. In each case, the stock was topped up back to eighteen cases.

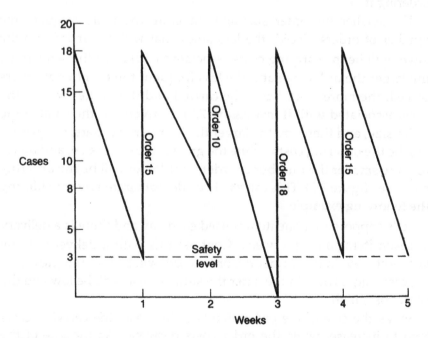

Figure 7.1 Periodic order (same order period – different order)

Economic order quantity (EOQ)

This system uses a formula to decide in what quantities materials should be ordered to ensure the minimum possible cost. It is not the intention to go into the formula here, but it would be useful to look at the underlying implications. If you are interested in seeing how the formula works in more detail you should read any book specializing in managing materials.

In order to be able to arrive at the EOQ it is necessary to have the following information available:

- An estimate of how many items are used
- How much each costs
- How much each order costs to place
- How much it costs to have the item in stock (as a percentage of the item cost)

The basis of the formula is that there are costs that are associated with carrying the item in stock, while there are other costs which relate to each order that is placed.

The total cost associated with the item can be reached by adding together the costs relating to carrying it and the costs relating to ordering it.

The smaller the order size and therefore the more frequent the number of orders placed, the less stock that will be carried and the lower will be the carrying costs associated with it. At the same time, the larger the order size and the less frequent the number of orders placed, the more stock has to be carried and the higher will be the costs associated with it (see figure 7.2). Conversely, the smaller the order size, and therefore the larger the number of orders, the greater will be the ordering costs, while the greater the order size, and there-fore the smaller the number of orders, the lower will be the ordering costs (see figure 7.3). This can easily be demonstrated by considering the following example.

Let's suppose that one item is used each day and there is a delivery of seven items once per week. Contrast this with a delivery of one item each day. In the former the order costs will be low and the carry-ing costs high, while in the latter the storage costs will be low and the order costs high.

So, as the size of the orders tends to increase, the carrying costs tend to increase, while the order costs decrease. As the size of the orders decrease then the order costs increase while the carrying costs decrease.

The formula allows one to find the order quantity at which the total

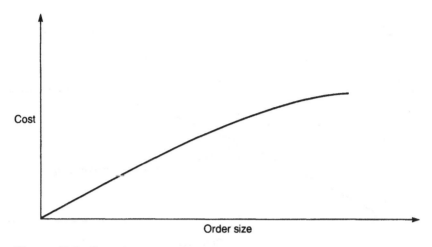

Figure 7.2 Carrying cost

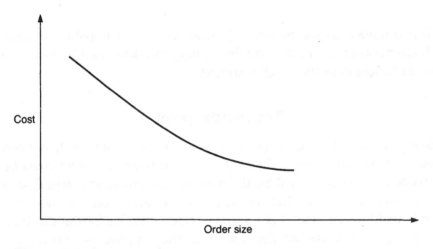

Figure 7.3 Ordering cost

cost is lowest. This is where the total cost of placing the orders and the cost of carrying the stock are equal (see figure 7.4).

The EOQ formula presents a number of problems. A number of assumptions have to be made which might not correspond to the reality of the actual workplace. These might include:

- assuming the demand is steady (which is rarely the case)
- assuming the item would cost the same whatever quantity was purchased, thus ignoring discounts for larger quantities.

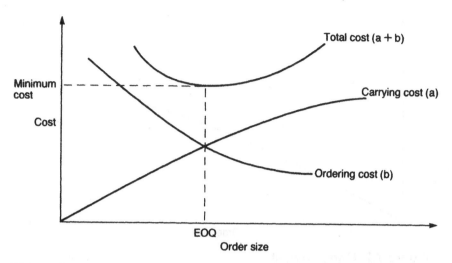

Figure 7.4 Total cost

The formula is useful, however, in studying the relationship between different order quantities, and fine-tuning can take place to cover the other factors once the EOQ is known.

The reorder point

Many organizations use a reorder point to ensure that they do not run out of a particular item. They set a level at which the item must be reordered. This level will be the average amount of the item that is used within the time that the item takes to arrive once it has been ordered (the lead time). Let's suppose, then, that we look at our local shop again and assume this time that the supplier has no regular delivery, but responds to orders within three days.

The reorder level will be the amount of cases that the shop owner expects to sell within that lead time of three days. However, where a safety stock is required, the reorder level will be the expected usage within the lead time, plus the safety stock.

In this situation the reorder level will be seven cases (he uses fifteen in a week so he will use approximately seven in three days) plus a level of safety stock. Let's assume two cases are required as a safety stock (because he only has to wait three days for a delivery, not seven as in the periodic order).

The reorder level will therefore be the expected usage (seven) plus the safety stock (two): a total of nine.

The actual number ordered will depend upon a number of factors and may well be decided by using the EOQ formula that was discussed earlier. In our example there may well be a limiting factor, such as the amount of space available to store the drinks. The store owner may therefore like to order a week's supply at a time; that is, fifteen cases. He will therefore order fifteen cases each time and will reorder whenever he gets down to nine. Three days after the order is placed he receives the fifteen cases.

His next order will be placed when he is again down to nine cases.

If the usage between the time he has placed the order and the time it is received is greater than expected, then he will have eaten into his safety stock by the time the order arrives. If it is less than expected, then he will have more on hand than usual once the order arrives. Either way, the next order is placed when he again reaches nine cases.

Thus, in this method, the order quantity remains fixed while the time between orders fluctuates.

The diagram in figure 7.5 shows an example of a reorder point system. In each case the order is for the same amount but it occurs at different frequencies. By the time the first order has been received the safety stock level of two has been reached. The next period is not so busy and sales are slow. Between the reorder point and the delivery of the order only two more cases are sold, so there are still eight on hand when it arrives, making a grand total of twenty-three on hand. However, a hot spell means that sales suddenly take off, the next reorder point is reached very quickly and the next delivery arrives just in time. In this situation he might start to re-examine both his order quantity and his safety stock.

When considering the lead time it is important to remember several points:

- the delivery may not arrive in the exact place that it is needed and may take time to move to the required location
- there is usually a requirement for the incoming order to be checked in some way to ensure that it is correct, and this may also take time
- the delivery may have to be entered into a computer-controlled system before use
- the time of day of the delivery is important, because a delivery in the late afternoon is no use if you need the items in the morning. A delivery the previous day would be necessary in this case.

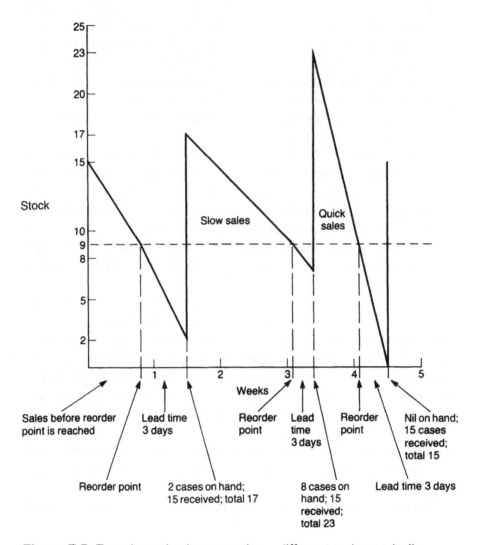

Figure 7.5 Reorder point (same order – different order period)

Whatever level is set for the reorder point it is necessary to have a system in place that will allow us to know when that point has been reached. This may range from sophisticated computer systems to a method of checking periodically to see what the current stock is. Some organizations which stack items one behind another have a physical marker which shows clearly when the reorder level has been reached.

We have mentioned safety (or buffer) stock several times already as a requirement to ensure that the stock does not run out because of the fluctuations that can occur in the demand.

SAFETY STOCK

The amount of safety stock that should be maintained is often difficult to assess. However, one of the most important factors to consider is how vital it is that stocks do not run out.

This involves a degree of risk which will vary from industry to industry. It would be intolerable for a sandwich bar to run out of butter as it would bring the operation to a standstill. On the other hand, if a travel agent ran out of one particular brochure it might not be quite so serious (though it might be serious for the particular tour operator concerned), unless people were asking for it specifically.

Where it is vital that stocks do not run out – and this may well be the case in some companies – it is possible to calculate the number that should be held with some accuracy.

This involves looking at the amount of the item used over a period and working out the average. As well as the average, the spread around this average can also be plotted. Using a statistical method known as 'standard deviation', it is possible to predict the amount of safety stock required to ensure that there is only a very rare possibility of running out.

We mentioned in chapter 5 the use of Pareto analysis when looking at problem-solving techniques. It can also be very useful in the control of inventory in conjunction with **ABC analysis**.

ABC analysis

Pareto discovered that in any group of items a relative few would account for a relatively high proportion of the group. This is often known as the eighty–twenty rule. It can be used in the control of inventory, because we can identify which items we most need to monitor. The first step is to list the items in order according to their total annual requirement value (ARV).

This is arrived at by multiplying the value of each item by the number of items used in a year. Table 1 shows a list of twenty items in descending order of their ARV. At the right-hand side is the cumulative total which shows each ARV added to the previous total.

This can then be plotted on a graph like that in Figure 7.6, which shows the cumulative total on the vertical axis and the list of items on

Table 1 Annual requirement Value (ARV)

Stock No.	Unit value	Units used	Annual requirement value	Cumulative
1	2,000	14	28,000	28,000
2	6,000	4	24,000	52,000
3	3,500	5	17,500	69,500
4	20	750	15,000	84,500
5	700	10	7,000	91,500
6	100	45	4,500	96,000
7	2	1,250	2,500	98,500
8	20	100	2,000	100,500
9	100	14	1,400	101,900
10	13	100	1,300	103,200
11	6	200	1,200	104,400
12	5	230	1,150	105,550
13	10	85	850	106,400
14	4	200	800	107,200
15	200	3	600	107,800
16	20	20	400	108,200
17	15	20	300	108,500
18	25	10	250	108,750
19	4	50	200	108,950
20	1	150	150	109,100

the horizontal axis. The cumulative total is then plotted against the items which demonstrate that just four of them (20 per cent of the items) account for some 77 per cent of the cumulative total. The next six items (30 per cent) make up the next 18 per cent of the total. The other ten items (50 per cent) make up just 5 per cent of the total.

From this we can allocate the items to the categories A, B and C. In the example A, items are those with an ARV of £15,000 and over; B items are those with an ARV of between £1300 and £15,000; C items are those with an ARV of less than £1300.

This is simply an example made up to illustrate the technique. The allocation of the items into the categories is a matter of managerial judgement, but it does show where we should concentrate our effort.

Clearly, if we ensure that all of the A items are tightly controlled,

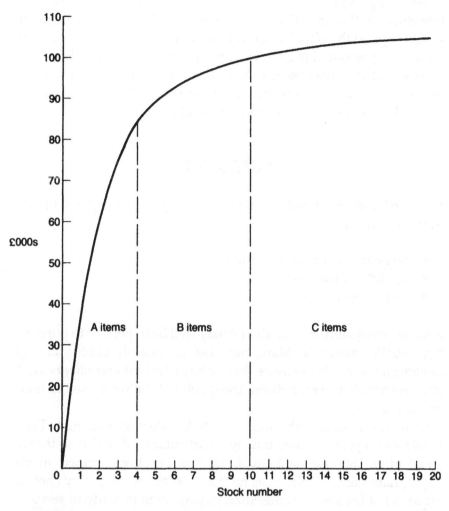

ABC Analysis

  4 items (20%) make up 77% of the total ARV – A items
  6 items (30%) make up 18% of the total ARV – B items
10 items (50%) make up 5% of the total ARV – C items

A = items with an ARV of £15,000 and over
B = items with an ARV between £1,300 and £15,000
C = items with an ARV below £1,300

Figure 7.6 Pareto curve of cumulative ARV

we are likely to be controlling nearly 80 per cent of the costs. B and C items would be subject to relatively less control.

Because of the huge costs that can be incurred by large organizations if they do not control the amount of inventory they maintain, it is becoming more and more common for computer systems to be introduced in this area. Complete systems can be used to evaluate the EOQ, to report the actual usage and the level on hand, to work out the number required and even to raise the order with the supplier.

Now that we have looked at how we should control the ordering of materials we need to consider what we should buy and where we should buy it. So let's now consider suppliers.

SUPPLIERS

Let's first consider what we should buy. This will depend upon a number of factors:

- the quality of the end product
- the skills of the staff
- the technology available

If the design quality is high, then it may well be important to purchase high quality materials. Marc, our chef is certainly aiming at high quality and so needs to ensure that he buys the best ingredients available. He has, however, reduced the quality of the wine used to make one of his sauces.

Clearly, the skills of the staff have to be taken into account. There would be no point in Marc buying a particular kind of fish so that he could offer Japanese sashimi, if he has not been trained in the appropriate skills. Similarly, as he is a good sweet and pastry chef, he makes all of his sweets rather than buying them in ready to serve.

The technology available is bound to have an important effect on the materials that are bought. If Marc has no microwave, then there is no point in buying anything which has to be specially prepared in it.

The same factors apply in any kind of organization. A local authority is not likely to buy the most expensive pens available to replenish stationery stocks; nor will it provide word processors for staff who have not been trained. A manufacturing company which uses fork-lifts to move materials around may well buy most of its stock on pallets.

So let's now look at how we should go about buying materials. The choice rests between using one supplier or a range of suppliers. There are a number of reasons why we might choose either of these courses. First, let's consider the advantages of a large range of suppliers:

- We can compare products from different suppliers to see which are the most appropriate for us.
- We can shop around for the best price.
- Competition may lead to a reduction of prices in general.
- We can look out for new products which may be of interest to us.
- If one supplier has problems relating to quality, we can easily switch to another.
- If one supplier goes out of business we can easily find another source of supply.

On the other hand, there are some advantages in dealing with a single supplier or a very small range of suppliers:

- The more orders we place with a single supplier, the more discount we are likely to obtain.
- We could work together on the design of particular components and share any savings due to the shared costs.
- It might be possible to improve the quality of supply due to the experience and knowledge that the single supplier gains.
- The supplier may act as a warehouse and store our components until we need them.
- If there is a shortage we are likely to be given priority.
- In respect of JIT systems it would be particularly desirable to deal with a single or a very small range of suppliers.
- The supplier can be given the same customer training as that received by the staff of the organization if he is likely to come into contact with customers.

Each organization will select the appropriate policy which will lead to their best advantage. Indeed they may use different policies according to the particular item of material. Some companies even go so far as to buy out the supplier in order to safeguard the supply of the particular item concerned.

Whichever method is chosen, it is important that a good relationship is built up between supplier and customer and that the relationship is built upon mutual trust.

There are three other methods of obtaining supplies that we ought to mention: tender, quotation and auction. These are very often used by government bodies as they ensure that a fair system operates and that the best possible price is obtained. They are also used in many other circumstances, including the buying and selling of property.

Tendering

Most organizations who use this system regularly have a list of suppliers whom they trust to provide a good service. They invite these companies to submit a price in a sealed envelope which must be received by a certain date. The organization usually, though not always, accepts the lowest tender.

The most important point to remember in this case is that the specification that is given for the particular item to be supplied must be the same for each company that is tendering. If a specification is changed it should be communicated to all the known tenderers.

Tendering is often used for obtaining the supply of services. Indeed, many local authorities are now subcontracting services that they used to provide in-house. They are usually allocated on a tender basis.

Once tenders are accepted they cannot usually be changed. They are usually initiated by the organization which wants to buy and may well involve large sums of money. It is aimed at obtaining the lowest price.

Quotations

Quotations are usually sought by people who want a particular service. They ask a company to indicate how much they will charge for a particular service or item. It is quite common for three or more quotations to be sought. Again it is important that the specification is the same in all cases. This method is often used by customers of jobbing firms like carpenters or electricians.

Again, it is the person who wants the supply who invites the quotations.

As a supervisor, you may well be involved in this method of obtaining supplies, especially if you are organizing a small alteration to your workplace. It is essential that other factors than price are considered.

THINK POINT

If you are arranging for work to be carried out by a contractor, what factors would you need to consider other than price?

First you would look for a firm with a good reputation so that you can be certain about the quality of the work. You would also want to be satisfied that they would still be in business later in case anything needed to be corrected or altered.

The method of carrying out the job would be important in that you might require the least amount of disruption to normal working arrangements.

With respect to our relationship with our customers, you might want a company who would treat any of your customers with whom they came into contact with consideration and politeness.

Auctions

Auctions are also aimed at obtaining the best price, but they are initiated by the seller. Bids are invited for items which are put up for sale. Auctions may involve prices starting low and going up until there are no more bids; or they may start high and be reduced until the first person makes a bid which is then accepted.

In any case there is usually a reserve placed upon the item, meaning that it cannot be sold unless that price has been offered. Organizations specializing in art or antiques may well use auctions to purchase their supplies. Builders too may purchase building plots or old barns for conversion in the same way.

The advantage for the purchaser is that it may well be possible to obtain a bargain since the price will reflect the desirability of the item to those who are attending. If there is little interest in the particular item it may well be sold very cheaply, subject to its reserve being reached.

Auctions can be very useful for the one-off purchase, but there is no contact between seller and buyer. It therefore is only a suitable method in certain circumstances. Someone starting up a new small business may well find an auction of second-hand office furniture to be particularly attractive.

Where to buy, therefore, is very much a matter for the particular organization concerned and will depend upon the particular circumstances at the time. Relationships with suppliers are important and are worth developing. Remember, as far as your customers are concerned, you are a supplier. So treat your suppliers the way you would like to be treated by your customers.

Finally, just as we have internal customers so we also have **internal suppliers**.

INTERNAL SUPPLIERS

Until recently it was automatic for an organization to use its own in-house services if they were available. Now, however, much more attention is being paid to the costs of such services with the result that competitive quotations from outside suppliers are often sought. In many cases, the in-house services are subcontracted to outside companies as we mentioned earlier in the case of local authorities. Training is one particular activity that is being handed over more and more to outside specialists. Manufacturing companies too may well decide to buy a component that they previously made themselves if there are advantages in doing so.

SUMMARY

Supervisory Management Standards:

Unit 2 Contribute to the planning, monitoring and control of resources
Element 2.1 Plan for the use of resources
2.2 Monitor and control the use of resources

Inventory consists of materials used by the organization and includes:

- raw materials
- finished goods used as inputs
- materials used for maintenance
- spares
- work in progress
- finished stock ready for the customer.

It is important that an organization is aware of the costs of holding inventory, and ensures that all inventory that is maintained is justified.

Standardization is a way of reducing the need to hold inventory.

When planning the control of materials it is necessary to distinguish between dependent items and independent items.

Dependent items are those whose usage will depend directly upon the usage of another item. Independent items do not have this direct relationship.

'Just in time' is a system which seeks to minimize the amount of materials held by the organization. It relies very heavily on quality, since any breakdown is likely to stop the whole production process. A predictable demand is also necessary.

We have considered three ways of controlling the ordering of stocks:

- periodic
- economic order quantity
- reorder point

Safety stock may be necessary to ensure that supplies do not run out.

ABC analysis is a useful method of ensuring that we focus on those items which are likely to make up most of our costs.

Suppliers are very important. A decision may have to be made as to whether the organization uses a single supplier or a range of suppliers for a particular item.

Chapter 8
Managing the Working Environment

Supervisory Management Standards:

Unit 1   Maintain services and operations to meet quality standards

Element 1.1 Maintain services and operations

        1.2 Maintain the necessary conditions for an effective and safe working environment

In this chapter we will be focusing on how we can ensure that the working environment allows our team to produce their best efforts. Element 1.2 of the Management Standards is particularly relevant as it covers most of the issues we will be discussing.

We will consider the working environment in two aspects:

1 Giving people equipment to help them
2 Maintaining a safe workplace

Let's look first at how we can help people to be more effective in their jobs by providing them with tools and equipment.

PROVIDING EQUIPMENT

Let's look at some of the equipment that we use in our jobs every day:

- notebook
- diary

- telephone/fax
- staplers
- list of telephone numbers

All of these items are fairly common and make life easier for us. In fact it is unlikely that we could do our job effectively without them. We just need to remember what it is like if we start a new job and the previous jobholder has not left a list of regular telephone contacts. However, it is surprising how often we just accept that a piece of equipment does not happen to be available in the workplace and we do things the hard way. How often have you used pieces of scrap paper rather than a notebook, with the result that you have notes lying around in various places where they can easily be lost?

Have you ever thought that you could really do with a telephone being installed in a particular place but have done nothing about it?

The trouble is that we grow to accept the way we are working and stop looking out for things that could make life easier.

THINK POINT

Can you think of any piece of equipment that could be obtained to help you and your staff to perform their jobs more effectively?

If you can't come up with anything it may be because you haven't really given enough thought to it.

Is it really necessary for people to lift that heavy case, or is there a piece of equipment that could help?

Do your staff have to use a messenger service to transport urgent papers to your customer? Would the installation of a fax machine be cheaper and easier?

Would a printed form save a lot of time in respect of routine matters that have to be reported?

Should your delivery driver be provided with a spare pair of spectacles in case he breaks those he is wearing?

The problem is that we readily accept what we already have and tend not to allocate time to the consideration of how jobs might be carried out more effectively. We looked at a problem concerning the use of a photocopier in chapter 4, where it was clear that a reallocation of working methods would be beneficial. There are many simple changes that can be made that do not involve a lot of expense. One of the most common sights in an office is the amount of paper lying around, on top of desks and filing cabinets. This is not only inefficient, it is also a fire hazard, which we will consider in more detail later. The situation can be improved by finding out why there is so much paper lying about and doing something about it. For example, the filing cabinets may be too small and the purchase of another one may be justified. Or they may be full of outdated files that can be destroyed if time was taken to sort them out. Or there may not be enough trays for papers to be stored on top of desks. These are all fairly simple solutions and unlikely to be expensive.

It is important that the right piece of equipment is obtained to suit the particular situation. It would not be necessary to provide a very sophisticated calculator for someone who has to make only simple calculations.

It may not be within your authority to buy a particular piece of equipment, but this does not stop you identifying what is required and presenting a case to your boss recommending that it be obtained. How to present information is covered in *In Charge, Managing Finance and Information.* It may seem that you haven't any time available to do this, but a small amount of effort in this respect may lead to the introduction of equipment or procedures that will save a lot of time later on.

Once the right piece of equipment has been obtained we need to ensure that proper training is given in its use. The amount of training necessary will vary according to the particular situation and the individual concerned. It may range from showing someone how to use a calculator in a matter of minutes, to arranging a training programme for staff to operate a newly computerized reservation system in a travel agent.

We also need to consider the location of any equipment that is installed. Most offices that we walk into today have a vast range of equipment ranging from furniture to filing cabinets, photocopiers and personal computers. These have usually been built up over the years. As a new piece of technology becomes available and is seen to be justified, it is acquired and allocated a position and some staff to use it.

This often results in a rather haphazard arrangement of equipment, based more on what space has allowed than on any forethought about the user's effectiveness or convenience.

THINK POINT

Think about the last piece of equipment that was introduced into your workplace. How was the decision reached as to where it should be located?

It is not possible to reorganize the workplace every time a new piece of equipment is introduced, but some thought should be given as to where it will be most effective. Usually this is achieved by consulting the staff who are going to use it. Consideration needs to be given to such factors as:

- Will more than one person be using it?
- Does it need a power supply?
- How often will it be used?
- Is it used in conjunction with something else?

Although this seems straightforward enough, it is surprising the amount of discontent that is caused in workplaces because insufficient consideration is given to this issue. We have already considered in chapter 4 how we might design the breakfast kitchen in our hotel to provide the most convenient arrangement.

With the amount of new equipment available today it is very important to ensure that the working environment is safe for our staff to work in. Let's now look at how we can bring this about.

MAINTAINING A SAFE WORKPLACE

Let's consider the definition of the word 'accident' to be: 'an unforeseen event, usually having unpleasant consequences'. We need to bear this in mind as we call in at our hotel, where Philip Burden, the leisure centre manager, appears to have a problem.

Case Note 13

Philip was in his office when the telephone rang. It was an emergency. One of the customers who had been for a swim was climbing out by means of the ladder in the corner of the pool when it came away from the wall. He fell back and hit his arm on the side of the pool. The pool attendant on duty was quick to spot the danger, and quickly pulled him out of the water and had applied some first aid. His arm appeared to be broken. An ambulance was called and the customer was now on his way to hospital.

Philip sat and reflected upon what had happened. Could the accident have been avoided? What lessons could be learned?

Well, first we need to ask Philip whether this was really an accident in the way that we defined it earlier. Was it really unforeseen or should it have been expected? It certainly had unpleasant consequences for the customer. Can Philip claim that he maintains a safe workplace?

We've considered a definition of 'accident' so perhaps we should look at what we mean by 'safe'. The best way to approach this is to start by considering what the Health and Safety at Work Act 1974 (HASAWA) means by safe. It is not the intention here to reproduce the Act itself. However, we do need to consider some of its provisions because they will help us to focus our attention on the important things.

The Act deals with a whole range of issues, including:

- The responsibilities for safety within an organization
- Plant and machinery
- Handling, storage and transport of materials
- Safe working conditions, including access and egress
- Training and information for employees to ensure their safety

The Act also covers first aid arrangements and emergency procedures; and deals with the introduction of safety representatives and safety committees.

In addition the Factories Act 1961 and the Offices, Shops and Railway Premises Act 1963 (OSRP) contain requirements in respect of the working environment, including:

- temperature and ventilation
- lifting
- toilet and washing facilities
- space
- cleanliness

- floors, passages and stairs
- protective clothing
- washing, eating and drinking facilities

Some of the provisions of the Factories Act and the OSRP Act have been replaced by legislation introduced at the beginning of 1993. In fact six new regulations have been introduced. They are as follows.

Management of health and safety at work regulations 1992

This is aimed at encouraging employers to take a more systematic approach to health and safety matters. The new regulations stipulate that employers should carry out an assessment of the risks to their employees and to anyone else affected, including members of the public and visitors to the premises. They also have to carry out any measures that appear to be necessary as a result of the risk assessment. Employers with five or more employees will also have to record any significant findings of the assessment and any measures they have taken. Such employers already have to provide a written statement of their health and safety policy.

The 1974 Act already lays down that responsibilities for observing its provisions apply both to employers and employees, and makes it clear that failure to carry them out may constitute a criminal offence. Both employers and employees may be prosecuted for such offences.

The new regulations also refer to the duty of employees to abide by safety procedures and to report any dangers that they observe.

Provision and use of work equipment regulations 1992

This regulation covers a broad range of equipment, from small tools to whole plants. It is concerned with every aspect of use:

- starting
- stopping
- maintenance
- operation
- safeguards
- suitability for the purpose
- training of staff to operate it

Manual handling operations regulations 1992

This contains a new approach and will require an employer to avoid manual handling wherever possible. So the starting point is not 'how many people do we need to move it?', but 'Does it need to be moved at all?' And if it is necessary, then the next consideration should be 'Is there any mechanical equipment that can be used to do the job?'

If manual movement is found to be necessary, an assessment should be carried out and recorded unless it is very simple. The assessment should cover a range of factors:

- weight
- shape
- size
- where it is to be handled
- the individual doing the handling and the posture required

The legislation applies to any movement and not just lifting.

Workplace (health, safety and welfare) regulations 1992

This regulation covers many of the aspects of the working environment previously contained in the Factories Act and the OSRP Act. It refers to requirements in four broad areas:

- The working environment, including temperature, ventilation, lighting, space, seating arrangements
- Safety, including access and egress, windows, doors and floors
- Facilities such as toilets and basins. It also refers to rest areas (free from tobacco smoke) and facilities for pregnant women and nursing mothers
- Housekeeping, including the maintenance and cleanliness of facilities and the removal of waste materials

Personal protective equipment at work (PPE) regulations 1992

This regulation relates to the use of all protective equipment, from clothing to eye and head protection. It also covers equipment used to increase safety, such as high visibility vests, safety harnesses and life jackets. The regulations also require the employer to

- assess the risks to ensure that the protective equipment is suitable

- maintain, clean and replace it
- ensure that adequate training is given so that it is properly used.

Health and safety (display screen equipment) regulations 1992

This is a new regulation which relates to the use of display screen equipment. Using display screens is not considered to be high risk, but can lead to physical problems such as eye fatigue or mental stress.

Although some of the out-of-date laws are being replaced, the more modern laws, such as the Control of Substances Hazardous to Health Regulations 1988 (COSHH), will be kept in place. The requirements of these regulations include the necessity for employers to make an assessment of risk associated with any hazardous substances and carry out the appropriate action that needs to be taken. (The source used for this information is: *New Health and Safety at Work Regulations*, published by the Health and Safety Executive.)

While the information above should be useful in giving you some general guidance concerning the various acts, you should consult the appropriate regulations for further details to enable you to carry out the provisions in full.

Health and Safety legislation also covers the appointment of safety representatives and the establishment of Safety Committees to represent the workforce in these matters.

In order to ensure that the organization is meeting its responsibilities under the various Acts it is necessary to carry out safety audits and inspections. The audit will identify those areas that are a possible source of danger, while the inspection will be carried out to ensure that any dangers that arise are corrected as soon as possible.

Inspections should be both routine, to ensure that a regular examination of the workplace is carried out; and random, to spot any hazards that arise in-between the regular inspections. A systematic procedure should be established for the reporting of any hazards that occur during the day-to-day working, and this should be indicated in the policy statement. People should be encouraged to report anything that they feel to be unsafe rather than holding back because they feel embarrassed that it may lead to production time being lost.

This is a real problem that supervisors face. There may well be times when they face a conflict between the demands of production and the need to lose time because a particular machine is not in a safe condition. However, under the terms of the Act the supervisor may well be found personally negligent if he or she takes no action and allows an unsafe situation to continue.

The legislation also covers the provision of trained first aid staff, first aid equipment and emergency procedures.

Let's now go back to the leisure centre and see whether Philip really is maintaining a safe working environment.

Case Note 14

Philip considered the situation. He had spoken to Bill, the pool attendant on duty. He was concerned to find out what had happened. It seemed that the ladder had simply come off its moorings without any warning; a complete accident.

Philip was not so sure. He asked when it had last been checked. Bill didn't know for certain. The pool had been emptied some four months ago for cleaning and had been closed for a week while maintenance was carried out. Philip thought for a moment. There should be a record of whether any inspection of the ladder had been carried out at that time. Bill shook his head. 'They only report it if they find something wrong. But surely we can assume that if nothing was reported then everything was OK, can't we?'

'Can we?' replied Philip, who was growing uneasy.

He reached into the drawer and rummaged through some files, emerging with a thin one that didn't look very promising. He looked at the last record of maintenance carried out. Sure enough, it told him what had been put right but didn't point to anything else that had been checked.

'When did we last have a safety inspection Bill?'

'Oh, I can't remember. You know we've been understaffed here for so long since Ken left that we haven't really had a chance to carry one out.'

'Who's the safety rep then?'

'Ken was', replied Bill.

Well, do we still think that this is an accident?

THINK POINT

Write down what you think has gone wrong in the leisure centre.

It's beginning to look as though there were a number of things that were not being carried out in the safest possible way. However, let's start by looking at the good points:

- Bill, the pool attendant, was trained in first aid and was able to handle the emergency in the first instance. In fact, all of the leisure centre staff are trained in first aid and a list is available on all of the hotel notice boards.
- The ambulance was called right away according to the emergency plan that is also on each staff notice board.
- Bill had informed all of the other leisure centre staff on duty about the situation and had closed the pool to allow: the ladder to be removed and roped off, and warning notices erected; the other ladders to be checked by the maintenance subcontractors who had been called and had attended very promptly – they were now in the process of carrying out repairs.
- Philip had a stock of accident report forms (which were standard throughout the hotel) and was filling one in showing the exact circumstances of the accident. This would be important for any future investigation. There may well be a claim for compensation from the customer.
- There used to be a safety representative.

Well, so much for what went right. Now let's look at what went wrong:

- There is a responsibility for ensuring the health and safety of all visitors to the premises. Clearly this did not happen.
- There is no record of what has been checked, only of what has been put right.
- There has been no safety inspection of the premises for at least four months, so there may be other 'accidents' waiting to happen.

- In fact, there has not even been a safety representative for the same period of time.

Case Note 15

The telephone rang and Philip picked it up. It was Eileen, one of the other pool attendants. She had been with him only a couple of weeks and had been employed as a replacement for Ken.

'Philip, you know the ladder that came away and caused the accident? You *did* get my note about it didn't you?'

'What note?'

'The one I left in your tray.'

'What did it say? '

'Well, one of our customers mentioned to me that the ladder seemed a bit wobbly. You weren't in so I left you a note about it, the day before yesterday.'

Philip started to rifle through the papers in his in tray and came across a scribbled note written in pencil.

'I've got it now,' he said.

His heart sank.

The situation is actually worse than it seemed at first. It now appears that this was an accident that could have been prevented.

THINK POINT

What lessons can be learned from this failure in communication?

Let's look at some of the issues raised here. First, Eileen clearly did not realize the seriousness of the situation. She had only been with the hotel for a couple of weeks. How much training had she been given?

Case Note 16

Philip thought for a moment. He hadn't really been able to spend much time with her since she arrived, but she had the necessary life saving qualifications and she gave a good account of herself at the interview, so he had assumed that she would be able deal with such problems. He looked at the roster. Her training had consisted of only one day spent with one of the other pool attendants, Bill as it happened, and then Bill had gone off sick and she had carried on on her own. Philip remembered that she seemed to know what she was doing; and after all, safety is really only common sense, isn't it?

'Bill, did you stress the importance of dealing with potential hazards immediately?'

'Hold on, I assumed that you had told her about all that. My job was to show her the ropes. Safety is your responsibility!'

It's quite clear that the ladder should have been put out of use immediately and repairs carried out. However, Eileen felt that she had done her duty by reporting it. After all, no one had been injured had they? She had not been told of the appropriate procedures and Philip had not carried out all of his responsibilities towards her as far as training was concerned.

So the real problem lies in the way it was reported, which was not a suitable method for this type of situation. A scribbled message put in someone's tray in the hope that it will be taken as urgent is clearly not appropriate.

What had happened when Eileen was on duty was in fact an incident. Let's consider a definition of 'incident': 'An occurrence that is out of the ordinary and which may result in an accident, but does not.'

Incidents are usually the first indication that an accident is about to happen. They act as a warning sign that our procedures are not good enough and that an accident is imminent. They are ignored at our peril.

In industries in which safety is a paramount consideration (e.g., the airline and maritime transport industries), a close inspection is carried out of any incidents that arise. All cases of near misses in the air, for example, are investigated thoroughly in order to find out whether the underlying cause has any wider implications for air safety.

The situation may be the subject of a public enquiry if it is considered to be sufficiently serious. Incidents involving nuclear power, for example, are particularly sensitive issues.

If we are to ensure the safety of everyone in the workplace our procedures should cover the management of incidents as well as accidents. The Management Standards (element 1.2) refer to potential breaches of the health and safety requirements.

We have mentioned in a number of places in this chapter that there is a responsibility for ensuring that such items as plant, machinery and equipment are kept in a safe condition. One of the best ways of achieving this is to carry out regular maintenance.

MAINTENANCE

As everyone knows from the time they buy their first car, if the engine is to be kept running we must apply a little oil periodically. If we want to be sure that all parts of the engine continue to work efficiently and safely, we will usually follow the manufacturer's recommendations and have it serviced at a garage at the specified intervals with the specified maintenance measures being carried out each time.

This involves us in two types of cost:

- the price charged by the garage for the work carried out
- the loss of the use of the car for the period of maintenance

However, there are alternatives to this and we can reduce the costs in the following ways:

- We can save the cost of the oil and the effort involved by not carrying out the task at all. Eventually, the engine may seize up completely and we will need to call the garage to come and repair it, *if* they can! The car may well be out of use for several days and the engine may even be beyond repair.
- Or we can have the engine serviced at time intervals greater than those recommended by the manufacturer, or have less work done than they specify. In short, we can reduce the amount of maintenance carried out. The risks of a failure are fewer than if we don't have the engine serviced at all, but greater than if we have the full service requirements carried out.

The question is, which of these courses of action is the most desirable? Or perhaps we should say 'most practicable', because many things that are desirable may not be so easy to put into practice.

There are two aspects that we will consider here: safety gained through maintenance; and cost-effectiveness of maintenance.

Safety gained through maintenance

In our example of the car above, we need to consider not only our own safety but that of other people too. What happens if the breakdown occurs on a busy motorway while we are driving at high speed? The consequences could be very serious for other road users if an 'accident' occurred.

We can apply this situation quite easily to the workplace. If plant and machinery are not properly maintained in accordance with the manufacturer's specifications they may easily become unsafe for people to use. This could well lead to the occurrence of injuries or even fatalities.

It is the responsibility of the supervisor to ensure that this does not happen.

Cost-effectiveness of maintenance

There is a continual tension between the requirements of carrying on with production and those of carrying out maintenance.

As we saw in the example of our car above, the result of reducing or ignoring maintenance altogether can be greater inconvenience and even higher costs.

This tension is best considered by looking at the overall costs of maintenance and repairs. In order to do this we need to account for all of the costs:

- costs of employing (or subcontracting) maintenance and repair staff
- costs of spare parts including ordering and carrying costs
- costs of any plant required to carry out maintenance
- costs associated with interference to production (downtime)
- costs of replacement if necessary

Generally speaking, the more planned and preventative maintenance (PPM) that is carried out, then the fewer breakdowns should be the result.

So as the costs of PPM increase, the costs of breakdowns are likely to decrease; while as the costs of PPM decrease the costs of breakdowns are likely to increase. It is a matter of judgement in obtaining the best possible balance between them. Safety issues should, however, be regarded as overriding the economic issues.

We mentioned earlier the distinction between practicable and desirable. Most organizations see the economic advantages of PPM. Indeed, many have a detailed plan to ensure that all of the maintenance schedules are met. The problems usually occur in actually carrying out the plan.

If there is a breakdown, there is no choice but to have the equipment repaired, and production may well stop until the repair is completed.

However, with PPM there is always a choice. The particular item is not broken and can usually be used for some time longer, especially if it has not become dangerous (this can be confirmed by an inspection). The demands of production may require that the machine be kept in service and miss its planned PPM appointment.

The danger usually occurs when the appointments for PPM are routinely suppressed because they interfere too much with production demands.

The result is that maintenance staff become 'firefighters', in that instead of maintaining the machines they simply respond to calls to attend them once they have broken down, or when an accident has occurred. Eventually, the number of breakdowns increases until they surpass the capacity of the maintenance staff to deal with them.

Where the same staff are used for maintenance and breakdown repair, it may be the staff themselves who become the scarce resource rather than the machine. They may be considered too valuable to be allowed to leave the production area to deal with routine maintenance elsewhere. Time might be lost.

THINK POINT

Does your department have a schedule for routine maintenance to be carried out in respect of any plant or equipment? Do you keep to this schedule?

Remember that plant and equipment does not mean only large machines in a manufacturing company. It covers the safe use of small items of electrical equipment too. Your office may have a contract for your word processors or photocopiers to be maintained.

It is important that records are kept of what has been inspected, as well as of what has been repaired or replaced.

As a supervisor you need to bear in mind that the costs of one accident – in respect of the misery it may cause to the people involved, the loss of reputation to your organization and the financial implications of compensation to victims – are likely to outweigh any of the efficiency arguments we have mentioned above.

Case Note 17

Philip looks up from the accident report form at the empty pool where the workmen are just finishing the repairs to the ladder, and ponders on what the headlines might be next morning in the local newspaper.

If we look back to chapter 2, there was an incident with a burning toaster in the breakfast kitchen of the hotel. It is questionable as to whether the toaster had been inspected recently, as the dangerous state it was clearly in had not been detected. A small piece of equipment could have been responsible for a major accident.

On the other hand, not all of the procedures in the hotel are failing to meet the necessary standards. The fire alarm system was working and the sprinklers did come into operation. At a subsequent investigation into the incident it was found that there were in fact complete records of inspections of the fire equipment. All fire extinguishers were found to be within their dates of effectiveness.

And, not least, there were records of fire drills that had been carried out, the latest having taken place only three weeks ago. So practice had indeed made perfect.

SUMMARY

Supervisory Management Standards:

Unit 1   Maintain services and operations to meet quality standards
Element 1.1 Maintain services and operations
          1.2 Maintain the necessary conditions for an effective and safe working environment

It is important that staff are provided with the appropriate equipment to enable them to carry out their jobs effectively.

Along with the provision of equipment, consideration needs to be given to

- who will use it
- where it will be used
- the necessary training to ensure that it is used properly

It is the employer's responsibility to provide a safe workplace for the staff and anyone else who is affected by the organization's activities.

Regular inspections and planned maintenance are essential to ensure that a safe workplace can be provided.

Chapter 9
Personal Competences

The personal competences most closely allied to the key role of operations are those connected with 'planning to optimize the achievement of results'. This is broken down into three areas as follows:

1.1 Showing concern for excellence
1.2 Setting and prioritizing objectives
1.3 Monitoring and responding to actual against planned activities

The other personal competences:

2 Managing others to optimize results
3 Managing oneself to optimize results

are covered in the *Managing People* volume, and

4 Using intellect to optimize results

is covered in the *Managing Finance* volume.

In Charge approaches the personal competences in the form of an *action plan*. When considering personal competences you should ask yourself:

- How well do I handle this area of personal competence?
- How could I handle it better?
- How does it relate to my functional competence at work?

In the preceding chapters of this volume we have looked at the operations process in some detail. The three areas of personal competence relating to this volume focus on three very fundamental aspects:

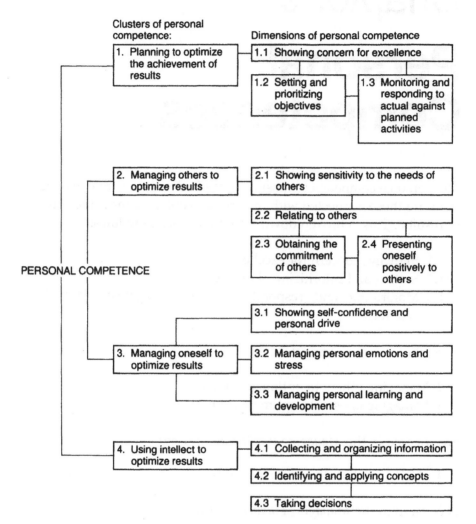

Figure 9.1 The MCI Personal Competence Model
Permission from MCI.

- Making sure that the future is planned and that everyone knows what the objectives are.
- Doing things to a high standard.
- Looking at what has happened and taking any necessary corrective actions.

We met these issues in chapters 3, 4 and 5 respectively.

1.1 Showing concern for excellence

Excellence means doing things to the standard expected by our customers, or even better. However, in order to be able to meet this ideal we and our staff need to know exactly what this standard is. It should be stated exactly, and not in vague terms, so that people know when they have achieved it.

THINK POINT

Do you always ensure that your staff know the standards expected of them and that they can be sure when they have achieved the standards?

Consider the following questions:

- Do you set yourself high standards?
- Do you try to improve your own performance?
- Are others really aware of the standards you expect?
- Do you set an example to others?
- Are you aware of any barriers to achieving excellence?
- Can you use change as a means of improving standards?

Action plan

Consider three things that you can personally do to raise the standards achieved by your staff.

1.2 Setting and prioritizing objectives

As we saw in chapter 3, it is vital that people are aware of what they have to achieve. After all, if they don't know what their objectives are, how can they be expected to achieve them. Objectives should wherever possible be agreed with your staff, rather than imposed, and they should be

- clear
- measurable
- achievable

However, it is also important that when objectives are set for your staff they are given priorities in order that their time can be allocated to best advantage. If you want something done by this afternoon then make it clear what you want, rather than asking for it to be done as soon as possible.

THINK POINT

Consider the last time you set an objective. Was it clear, measurable and achievable? Did you set a deadline by which it should be completed?

Consider the following questions:

- Do you look ahead and plan for future needs and changes, not just for present needs?
- Can you identify future problems and plan for the 'what if' situations?
- How can you be sure that you are using your time and your resources (staff, money, materials etc.) to best advantage?
- Do you maintain the balance between differing objectives within the organization? For example:

    Company policy
    Departmental objectives
    Group objectives
    Individual needs
    The task

- Do you consult others to ensure that objectives are both achievable and challenging?
- How do you measure success?

Action plan

What steps do you personally need to take to ensure that your staff are absolutely sure of what you expect them to achieve?

1.3 Monitoring and responding to actual against planned activities

Now that you have set your standards and objectives and are sure that everyone knows what they have to do to achieve success, it is important that you monitor what is actually happening. It may be necessary to take corrective action to put things back on track. In any case, even if everything is going according to plan, it will be necessary to give your staff some feedback so they know that you are satisfied with their performance.

Monitoring how any particular project is going will satisfy your own concerns about how it is progressing, and will reassure your staff that you are interested in the outcome.

THINK POINT

Have you ever had the feeling that things were not going quite according to plan, but have left the situation alone in the hope that it would come right in the end?

Well, if you're very lucky it might have done. However, it is more probable that things didn't improve and you wish that you had taken some action earlier. Corrective action needs to be taken as soon as things are seen to be going wrong, rather than left until the final product is rejected.

Consider the following questions:

- What monitoring techniques are you using for controlling your resources?
- Do you encourage others to assess their own performance against the objectives they have been set?
- Do you modify and change objectives if they become unrealistic or unattainable because of other factors outside your control?

- Do you look for and identify problems which would prevent the objectives being met, and replan accordingly?

Action plan

Look at the measures you are currently using to monitor progress within your workplace. Are you happy that you find out what is going wrong *in time* to put it right?

This concludes *Managing Operations*, the second volume of *In Charge: A Competence Approach to Supervision and First Line Management*. It is a starting-point for considering the underpinning knowledge needed by the competent supervisor/first line manager. It will not make you competent: no book can do that. But it has attempted to provide you with the knowledge needed to understand the Management Charter Initiative Standards for Supervisors and, from that knowledge, considered within your work situation, can flow competence.

References

Drucker, P. (1968): *The Practice of Management*. London, Heinemann.

Hill, T. (1991): *Production/Operations Management*. Hemel Hempstead, Prentice Hall.

Kotler, P. (1991–2): *Marketing Business*. December 1991–January 1992.

Peters, T. J. and Waterman, R. H. (1982): *In Search of Excellence: Lessons from America's Best-run Companies*. New York, Harper and Row.

Wild, R. (1985): *Essentials of Production and Operations Management*. London, Holt, Rinehart and Winston.

Further Reading

For a more detailed analysis of the Economic Order Quantity, you might like to read pages 423–7 of *Operations Management: Decision Making in the Operations Function*, by Roger G. Schroeder, McGraw–Hill, 1989.

The same book has an excellent section (chapter 16) on 'just in time' manufacturing.

If you are interested in finding out more about standard deviation, you will find the following book useful: *The Effective Use of Statistics: A Practical Guide for Managers*, by T. Hannagan, Kogan Page Professional Paperbacks.

How to use standard deviation in making decisions about safety stock can be found in *Production/Operations Management*, by T. Hill, p. 27.

Index

Printed and bound by CPI Group (UK) Ltd, Croydon, CR0 4YY

09/06/2025

14686146-0005